ANIMALS
PHOTOGUIDE

Text by John A. Burton

HarperCollins*Publishers*

HarperCollins*Publishers*

PO Box, Glasgow G4 ONB

First published 1996

Reprint 9 8 7 6 5 4 3 2 1 0

ISBN 000 470824 5

Typeset by TJ Graphics

Printed in Italy by Amadeus S.p.A

CONTENTS KEY

This book is designed as an introduction to the mammals, reptiles and amphibians of Europe, with all the major types illustrated. The general introduction describes each of the main groups, such as insectivores, bats, lizards or snakes, and a selection of species is illustrated and described in more detail.

Each of the groups is indicated by a small symbol at the top of the page, as follows:

Insectivores (Insectivora) (pp. 14–25)
Primitive mammals, mostly small, feeding on invertebrates, or occasionally small amphibians, reptiles or mammals

Bats (Chiroptera) (pp.26–47)
The only mammals capable of true flight. All European species feed on flying insects and spiders. Most hibernate

Rabbits and Hares (Lagomorpha) (pp.48–53)
Similar to rodents with which they were once classified. All have relatively long ears

Rodents (Rodentia) (pp.54–85)
The most numerous group of mammals in the world. All have characteristic large incisor teeth

Primates (pp.86–87)
Humans and their closest relatives. Only one species (other than humans) occurs in Europe

Carnivores (Carnivora) (pp.88–111)
Mostly predators, though some eat fruit or scavenge

Walrus and Seals (Pinnipedia) (pp.112–119)
Marine mammals spending most of their life in the water, but come to land or ice to breed

 Hoofed Mammals (Ungulata) (pp.120–139)
Generally large mammals with either a single hoof or divided into two

 Whales and Dolphins (Cetacea) (pp.140–151)
Entirely marine mammals, giving birth to their young at sea

 Salamanders and Newts (Caudata) (pp.152–167)
Tailed amphibians, very variable in their life cycles

 Frogs and Toads (Anura) (pp.168–187)
Tailless amphibians, all have aquatic larvae (tadpoles)

 Tortoises and Turtles (Testudines) (pp.188–199)
Shelled reptiles. The marine and fresh water species return to land to breed

 Lizards (Sauria) (pp.200–224)
Tailed reptiles showing a very wide range of body shape and colour; most lay eggs

 Amphisbaenian (p.225)
A worm-like reptile

 Snakes (Ophidia) (pp.226–250)
Limbless reptiles, some of which are venomous

SPECIES ENTRIES

The most widely used English names are given, followed by the scientific name, which is Latinised. The scientific name comprises two words, the generic name (which is always capitalised), followed by the specific name (which is never capitalised, even if it is based on a person's proper name). The generic name indicates closely related species, and is often abbreviated to its capital letter when repeated. A general description is followed by summary notes under the following headings:

Size	The measurements usually refer to the head and body, and the tail length when appropriate. In other species, such as bats, measurements are given for wingspan.
Habitat	The most common or typical habitat is described, however it should be taken into account that some species may occur in other similar habitats.
Food	A brief summary of the most usual foods eaten are given although many species may eat a much wider variety of related animals or plants. This depends largely on the particular species, and the availability of food supplies.
Range	This summarises where the species is most likely to be encountered within Europe. It is important to remember that a species is only likely to be found in suitable habitats within its range.
Similar species	Information is given on species that might be confused with the one being described. In some instances mention is also made of related species which are not illustrated.

LOOKING FOR WILD ANIMALS

Reptiles, amphibians and mammals, although widespread and often common, are generally more difficult to observe than birds. But a few useful tips may help you to find them.

Mammals

Most mammals are nocturnal, rarely emerging from their dens or roosts before nightfall. However, searching a garden at night, with a strong beam torch, will often reveal a noisy hedgehog snorting in the undergrowth. (When using a torch it is important to remember that the full beam should never be shone directly into the animal's eyes, but always slightly to one side.) Bats can frequently be seen in the twilight, although even experts find them almost impossible to identify precisely in flight. Mice, and even shrews, can be attracted to nocturnal feeding stations by putting out cat food, fishing maggots, seeds and berries. Any small table, similar to a bird table, can be adapted for this use, but it must be placed near the ground and close to shrubs and bushes. Once small mammals are used to a particular feeding place they will usually become accustomed to artificial light. Some mammals will even use bird nesting boxes, and sometimes will take over bird boxes during the winter months – it is always worth checking these carefully for wood mice and dormice.

Larger mammals, such as deer, ibex and wild sheep, require stealth, patience, and often a pair of binoculars to spot them across valleys or close to the horizon.

To see whales and dolphins you really need to be in a boat, and some of the smaller species will sometimes ride the bow wave of a boat. Larger whales are usually only glimpsed as their back breaks the surface of the sea, or you may be lucky enough to see their 'blow' – the water vapour of their breath.

Amphibians

Amphibians are relatively easy to see, and perhaps the best way is to visit ponds in which they breed in spring. But even if you do not manage to see them in the breeding season you may well find their larvae, or tadpoles. Amphibians can often be found by searching at dusk or after dark on a warm, wet evening, as this is the time they normally come out to feed. They are often found under outside lights, or you could use a torch to search for them. Amphibians and reptiles (and some small mammals) can also be found under logs, sheet iron or planks. But always remember to replace any of these hiding places exactly as you find them, and do not walk on iron sheeting or planks if you know there are animals underneath as your weight could easily damage them.

Reptiles

Most reptiles love basking in the sunshine, and the best time to look for them is when the sun is first beginning to really warm the ground. They are often very shy, scuttling away before you have a chance to get a good look. But if you note where you first saw them and return half an hour later, perhaps using binoculars to see them from slightly further away, there is a very good chance they will have returned to the same basking place.

ALWAYS LISTEN TOO

Listening can also lead you to animals. A gentle, continuous rustling in the undergrowth may indicate a snake slithering away. A short rustle, a pause, followed by another short rustling among dry leaves, often indicates a lizard. Frogs and toads have a variety of distinctive croaks, some loud, some very subdued. Bats emit high-pitched squeaks, only some of which are audible to humans, and even these tend to become inaudible as we grow older and our sense of hearing becomes less acute. Carnivores, however, are often quite noisy, particularly in the breeding season, and you will usually hear them even if you do not see them.

HANDLING ANIMALS

As a general rule it is best only to handle wild animals under the guidance of an expert. An expert will stress the importance of treating all wildlife with caution and will remind you that you must wet your hands before handling amphibians, and that you should wear gloves if you are handling most other animals. Some snakes are poisonous, and although human fatalities are extremely rare, a bite from them can be unpleasant. Similarly, while rabies in mammals is rare, and human fatalities even rarer, some mammals do carry diseases transmissible to humans. Particular care should be exercised when handling sick or injured animals.

The Habitats of European Wildlife

Arctic tundra

The Arctic is characterised by a very simple ecosystem with relatively few species. The vegetation is low, with dwarf willows and other short trees. Mammals of this region often have fur that is white in winter, to provide camouflage in the snow. Because they are cold blooded, most reptiles and amphibians are not well adapted to the Arctic, but the Common Lizard, Adder (both of which retain their eggs within the body and are able to incubate them by sunning themselves) as well as the Common Frog, all manage to breed within the Arctic Circle. Arctic Foxes, lemmings and voles all have populations which are often cyclical, numbers building up over several years then crashing when food becomes short.

Deciduous woodland

Much of Eastern Europe was once covered in deciduous woodlands, often with huge oaks, hundreds of years old. Remnants of these mighty forests are now reduced to a few isolated pockets in eastern Europe which means that the wildlife that depend on them is also much rarer than previously. Large mammals such as the Bison, Wolf and Wild Boar, as well as the Pine Marten, are found in the forests, and crevices and hollows in trees, as well as old woodpecker holes, provide ample roosting places for bats. Reptiles, such as the green lizards, occur in the more open areas and snakes, such as the Grass Snake, breed in rotting vegetation along the rivers. Beneath rotting logs amphibians as well as Slow Worms and small mammals may be found hiding in the damp soil.

Wetlands

Swamps and marshes once covered huge areas of Europe, but from the sixteenth century onwards the majority have been drained because they often provided fertile farmlands. In their original state, wetlands provide homes for a wide range of amphibians, particularly frogs and toads, and several species of snake, as well as mammals including Beaver, Otters and Mink. Many bats feed on the insects that infest wetlands, while terrapins and smaller mammals including Water Voles, Water Shrews and Harvest Mice are rarely found more than a few metres from water.

Mountains and coniferous forests

The mountain tops of Europe are still quite rugged, and although tourist development reaches almost all the peaks and summits, it is still possible to find relatively unspoiled valleys and slopes. Close to the snow line several small rodents, such as the Snow Vole, occur and the whistle of the Marmot is one of the characteristic sounds of the Alps in summer. More difficult to see, although their numbers are steadily increasing, are the Ibex and Chamoix. The Alpine Salamander overcomes the problem of the cold and the short summers by retaining its eggs within the body and giving birth to fully developed young.

Mediterranean and desert habitats

Around the Mediterranean there are many relatively dry habitats, and in parts of Spain, Italy and south-east Europe there are areas that qualify as deserts. It is in these drier habitats that several species of reptile abound. But if you want to observe them, remember that during the hotter months of the year, most species are only active at night or in the early hours of the day, and some may even aestivate (the summer equivalent of hibernation).

INTRODUCED ANIMALS

Several species only occur in Europe as a result of being introduced by humans. Sometimes they were introduced for food, sometimes as pets which subsequently escaped and bred, and for others there is no apparent reason. Raccoons, Musk Rat, American Mink and Bullfrog were all imported from North America. The Coypu originated from South America, the Axis Deer, Muntjac and Chinese Water Deer from Asia. The Barbary Ape, Genet, Mongoose, Porcupine and Chameleon all came from North Africa, and the occurrence of tortoises, tree frogs, hares and rabbits on many Mediterranean islands is almost certainly due to humans moving them around. Generally, the introduction of exotic animals is considered detrimental, since they often compete with native wildlife, and may also do considerable damage. The most damaging of all introductions are undoubtedly the rodents – House Mouse, Black Rat and Brown Rat originally came from Asia, and not only do they cause millions of pounds worth of damage every year, but they are also responsible for diseases such as the plagues that used to wipe out a large proportion of the human population.

CONSERVATION

Many of Europe's mammals, reptiles and amphibians have declined drastically in numbers and several species are now extremely rare. The original natural vegetation that covered Europe was vastly different from what now covers most of the region. Even the landscape of forty years ago was significantly more suitable for wildlife. From the Iron Age onwards the primeval forests and grassy savannahs were cleared to make way for agriculture, and at the same time the huge wild oxen (Aurochsen) were hunted to extinction. Many others mammals, such as Wolves and Bison, only survived in a few remote parts of Europe, and now need legal protection. Since World War II the onslaught of natural habitats has continued and the agricultural landscapes became increasingly sterile. Flower-rich meadows were 'improved' (with fertilisers) or ploughed, and pesticides and herbicides eliminated weeds and most invertebrates from the arable fields. Hedgerows were ripped out to create larger and larger fields, until most of the landscape of western Europe is little more than an inhospitable desert for wildlife. Not surprisingly the populations of many species have plummeted and are now only a fraction of their former numbers. Several species of bat are now endangered, and local extinctions of many species of mammal, reptile and amphibian have already occurred. These extinctions usually occur on the edges of their range – for instance, in Britain, where Sand Lizards, Smooth Snakes, several bats, and Natterjack Toad are among the most threatened species.

Most countries now have 'Red Data Books' for their wildlife, where threatened species are listed according to the risk of extinction. While hunting and other pressures may affect some species, there is little doubt that the wholesale destruction of natural habitats, such as marshes and forests, coupled with the intensification of farming, have had the most disastrous impacts on wildlife.

What You Can Do

The first step towards helping save wild animals and their habitats is to join an organisation dedicated to conserving them. In the British Isles there are many such organisations, some working at a local level and others regionally. The county Wildlife Trusts are involved in all conservation issues within their county, while national organisations, such as the Bat Conservation Trust, deal with a particularly threatened group of animals. Public libraries usually have directories of the major organisations, as well as the local ones, and the government bodies responsible for wildlife.

Having joined an organisation there are several ways you can help. Many offer opportunities for practical conservation activities, which could range from clearing overgrown ponds for amphibians, to putting roosting boxes in conifer plantations for bats. You could also take part in survey work for which even the inexperienced layman can help, with a minimum of training. These include keeping records of animals found dead on roads, dissecting owl pellets to see what animals they have been eating, or counting breeding frogs in a pond. Most Natural History societies are only too keen to recruit new, enthusiastic members of the public and they often organise get-togethers and field excursions to help beginners.

INSECTIVORES

Insectivores are primitive mammals, and some are probably very similar in appearance to the earliest known mammals. They are mostly small (the Pygmy White-toothed Shrew is one of the smallest mammals known, measuring 36-53 mm and rarely weighing more than 2 g), with the hedgehogs being among the largest known insectivores, growing up to 30 cm long and weighing up to 1.5 kg. As their name suggests, insectivores mostly feed on insects, but they also feed on other invertebrates such as earthworms and molluscs. Their teeth are usually rather simple pointed pegs that are suitable for holding their prey. The shrews have a very high metabolic rate and spend their lives alternately rushing around searching for food and sleeping; they are generally active both by day and night. Hedgehogs conserve energy by becoming torpid during the colder months (hibernating). The shrews are rarely seen, but their high-pitched squeaks are often heard, and moles are usually detected by their mounds of earth. Hedgehogs are all too frequently encountered as road casualties because, despite popular opinion, they have not learned to avoid cars, but roll up on their approach.

Hedgehogs are all too often encountered as road casualties

HEDGEHOG *Erinaceus europaeus*

The Hedgehog is easily recognised by its spines, which cover its back and sides and are erected by powerful skin muscles. Mainly active at dusk and dawn, it is often very noisy as it searches undergrowth for insects. It hibernates for up to 5 months in a nest usually made of leaves, and gives birth to 2–9 pink, soft-spined young in late spring or early summer. It sometimes has a second litter.

Size	Up to 30 cm, tail largely concealed.
Habitat	Mostly wooded areas including gardens.
Food	Insects, eggs, chicks and other young birds.
Range	Widespread and common over most of W Europe, including islands.
Similar species	Algerian Hedgehog (opposite).

ALGERIAN HEDGEHOG *Atelerix (Erinaceus) algirus*

This species is very similar to the more widespread Hedgehog (opposite). It is most easily distinguished by a parting in the spines on the forehead. It is usually paler, and also has proportionally longer legs. Like the Hedgehog, it is mostly active at night, and most likely to be seen as a road casualty. It does not hibernate.

Size	Up to 30 cm, including a short tail.
Habitat	Usually wooded areas, often gardens.
Food	Insects and other small animals.
Range	Confined to Mediterranean coastal regions of Spain, France and the Balearic Islands. More widespread in North Africa.
Similar species	Hedgehog.

PYRENEAN DESMAN *Galemys pyrenaica*

Best described as an aquatic mole, the Pyrenean Desman is well adapted to its aquatic life. It has webbed hind feet, water repellent guard hairs and a long, mobile snout, with valves in its nostrils. It is active by night and virtually blind. The single litter of about 4 young is born in a burrow in spring or early summer.

Size	Up to 16.5 cm, plus a tail of up to 15.5 cm.
Habitat	Fast-flowing mountain streams.
Food	Aquatic invertebrates and small fish.
Range	Confined to Pyrenees, NW Spain and Portugal at altitudes of 300–1,200 m.
Similar species	Water Shrew (p.23) is smaller and black. Water voles (pp.74 & 75) have blunt muzzles. Also rats (pp.77 & 78).

MOLE *Talpa europaea*

The Mole has a cylindrical body covered with short, dense black fur. It spends most of its life underground, tunnelling with its pink, spade-like front paws and pushing up molehills at intervals. It is solitary, except during the breeding season, and is active day and night throughout the year.

Size	Up to 15 cm.
Habitat	Grassland and woodland.
Food	Mainly earthworms, which it immobilises by biting off the front end, and other invertebrates.
Range	Widespread in Europe, except most of the Mediterranean, Spain, Portugal, Ireland and N Scandinavia.
Similar species	Two other European moles: Blind (or Mediterranean) Mole, *T. caeca*, and Roman Mole, *T. romana*.

COMMON SHREW *Sorex araneus*

The velvety fur is tri-coloured: brownish-black on the back, warmer brown along the sides and greyish-white on the belly. It is generally solitary, except in the breeding season when the female builds a nest of leaves and moss and produces 5–10 young (sometimes 2 litters a year). Active during a 24–hour period, it searches for food at three-hourly intervals. Shrews do not hibernate.

Size	55–85 mm, plus a tail of up to 47 mm.
Habitat	Most places with good ground cover.
Food	Insects, spiders, snails and other invertebrates.
Range	Throughout most of N and E Europe.
Similar species	Several closely related shrews are very difficult to identify in the field.

Pygmy Shrew *Sorex minutus*

This shrew is smaller than the Common Shrew (opposite), but with a proportionally longer and thicker tail; it is brown above and paler below. It usually lives in burrows made by other animals and builds a nest woven from dry grass. It is also often arboreal (tree-living), and is active both day and night. Up to 2 litters are born a year, each of 2–12 young.

Size	39–64 mm, plus a tail of up to 44 mm.
Habitat	Most places with ground cover.
Food	Woodlice and other invertebrates and insects.
Range	Widespread across most of Europe, except parts of Spain, Portugal and Mediterranean islands.
Similar species	Least Shrew, *S. minutissimus*, which is even smaller.

ALPINE SHREW *Sorex alpinus*

The Alpine Shrew is blackish-grey with only slightly paler underparts. Like other shrews, the fur is velvety, the snout long and pointed and the legs short. It generally occurs in mountain regions, at altitudes over 500 m up to the tree line; in winter it lives in tunnels beneath the snow.

Size	59–83 mm, plus a tail of up to 74 mm.
Habitat	Mainly coniferous forest, also alpine meadows and moorland, often near water.
Food	Snails, earthworms, insects and spiders.
Range	The Alps, and mountains of E Europe.
Similar species	Water Shrew (opposite) is larger and usually has a white underside.

WATER SHREW *Neomys fodiens*

The largest shrew, with blackish fur above and white underneath (although this varies and can be blackish), it has a silvery appearance under water. The tapering tail has a 'keel' of bristles along the underside that acts as a rudder, and the hind feet and toes are fringed with hair, which helps it swim and dive well.

Size	70–96 mm, plus a tail of up to 72 mm.
Habitat	Mostly wetlands, preferring clear lakes and slow-moving streams.
Food	Small aquatic animals including fish, frogs and newts; also shellfish and insects.
Range	Most of Europe, except much of Spain, Portugal and SE Europe.
Similar species	Miller's Water Shrew, *N. anomalus*, and Alpine Shrew (opposite).

PYGMY WHITE-TOOTHED SHREW *Suncus etruscus*

This is one of the smallest mammals in the world, and is very elusive. It has largish ears, reddish-brown upperparts, the tail is proportionally longer than other shrews and is 'whiskered'. It nests under stones, logs or tree roots and up to 6 litters are born each year, with 2–6 young in each litter.

Size	36–53 mm, plus a tail up to 30 mm. Rarely weighs more than 2 g.
Habitat	Wide variety of fairly dry, but well-vegetated habitats. Prefers sunny open scrub.
Food	Small insects, including grasshoppers, and spiders.
Range	Widespread in Mediterranean areas, also the Atlantic coast of France.
Similar species	Other species of white-toothed shrew.

LESSER WHITE-TOOTHED SHREW *Crocidura suaveolens*

The Lesser White-toothed Shrew is grey-brown above, sometimes with a reddish tinge, and paler below; it has a long, 'whiskered' tail. It nests under logs and stones and also in burrows – sometimes using those made by other animals. The single litter (occasionally two) has 2–6 young, born naked and helpless.

Size 49–78 mm, plus a tail of up to 50 mm.
Habitat Very variable, including coastal areas, scrub and gardens.
Food Insects and larvae; spiders and beetles.
Range Common and widespread in SE Europe, less common in France, Spain and Portugal. In the UK restricted to the Scilly Isles. Also in the Channel Islands.
Similar species Greater White-toothed Shrew, *C. russula*.

BATS

Bats are the only mammals capable of true flight. Although some tropical bats are large – with a wingspan of over 1.5 m – those found in Europe are all comparatively small. They range from the pipistrelles, with a wingspan of around 25 cm, up to the Greater Mouse-eared Bat with a wingspan of 45 cm. They are all insectivorous and all navigate by means of sonar. They emit high frequency sounds (much higher than the human ear can hear), and use the echo to pinpoint the position of their surroundings. This echolocation is extremely accurate and enables them to catch their prey, which is mostly relatively small insects. Bats are generally long-lived, many species living around 10 years in the wild, and some have lived for over 20 years. They mostly produce a single young, though twins are not uncommon in some species. Except in the extreme south of Europe, bats hibernate, often gathering in large colonies in caves. Nearly all Europe's bats are considered threatened. Their numbers have declined from a variety of causes that include disturbance during hibernation, poisoning from both agricultural insecticides and timber treatment in houses, and also destruction of roost sites in old trees.

Brown Long-eared Bat in flight

GREATER HORSESHOE BAT *Rhinolophus ferrumequinum*

This bat's name is derived from the flap of skin on its nose, which is shaped like a horseshoe and is often referred to as a 'nose-leaf'. The soft fur on its back is grey-brown, on the undersides it is white. It roosts in roof spaces, barns, mines and caves, and hibernates in colonies. The single young is born June–August. It is endangered throughout Europe.

Size	57–71 mm, plus a tail of up to 43 mm, and a wingspan up to 40 cm.
Habitat	Wooded countryside with suitable roosts.
Food	Mainly flying insects.
Range	Patchy distribution throughout Europe, as far north as S Britain and east to the C Russian states.
Similar species	Other species of horseshoe bat.

LESSER HORSESHOE BAT *Rhinolophus hipposideros*

One of the smallest bats in Europe, it has pointed ears. Its flight is erratic and fluttering and it frequently searches for food close to the ground, snatching insects from among rocks and branches. It gives birth to one young a year; in winter it hibernates singly or in small clusters, hanging from the roof.

Size	37–45 mm, plus a tail of up to 33 mm, and a wingspan of up to 25.4 cm.
Habitat	Wooded countryside; roosts in trees, outbuildings, caves and tunnels.
Food	Flying insects and spiders.
Range	Declining numbers in S and C Europe, also SW Britain and W Ireland.
Similar species	Other species of horseshoe bat.

DAUBENTON'S BAT *Myotis daubentoni*

These small bats are also known as Water Bats as they often hunt over water, skimming the surface in search of insects, and sometimes taking fish from the water. The fur is reddish-brown above, greyer below, and the feet are proportionally large. It roosts in attics and trees, and in winter usually hibernates underground in caves and tunnels.

Size	45–55 mm, plus a tail of up to 45 mm, and a wingspan of up to 27.5 cm.
Habitat	Open woodland and parkland, usually near water.
Food	Insects, mayflies and midges; occasionally fish.
Range	Throughout most of Europe, including parts of Great Britain and Ireland.
Similar species	Other *Myotis* bats.

POND BAT *Myotis dasycneme*

The Pond Bat is grey-brown above, greyish below and has large, sparsely haired feet. It is critically endangered, probably due to poisoning from timber treatment chemicals. It hibernates singly or in small clusters.

Size	57–68 mm, plus a tail of up to 53 mm, and a wingspan of up to 32 cm.
Habitat	Feeds in woodland and meadows; roosts in buildings, caves and cellars.
Food	Insects.
Range	E and C Europe, west to Belgium and NE France, north to Sweden and south to Slovakia.
Similar species	Long-fingered Bat, *M. capaccinii*, smaller and confined to Mediterranean areas, is distinguished by downyish hair on the wing, ear shape and large, bristled feet.

WHISKERED BAT Myotis mystacinus

The smallest *Myotis* bat, the Whiskered Bat has variable coloured shaggy fur which is dark to light brown above and greyer below. It often hunts over water and prefers to hibernate in damp cold places, such as caves and tunnels. A single young is born each year, in mid-June.

Size	35–48 mm, plus a tail of up to 43 mm, and a wingspan of up to 22.5 cm.
Habitat	Woodland and gardens; roosts in hollow trees and bat and bird boxes; hibernates in caves and cellars.
Food	Flying insects.
Range	Widespread over most of Europe, except Spain, Portugal and extreme north.
Similar species	Only differentiated from Brandt's Bat (opposite) in Europe in 1958.

BRANDT'S BAT *Myotis brandti*

A very small bat, almost identical in general appearance to the Whiskered Bat (opposite). For many years they were thought to be the same species, but Brandt's has a more reddish-brown tinge to the fur on the upperside. The only sure way of distinguishing the two species, however, is by a close examination of the teeth.

Size	41–53 mm, plus a tail of up to 46 mm, and a wingspan of up to 24.5 cm.
Habitat	Woodland and gardens; roosts in hollow trees and bat and bird boxes; hibernates in caves and cellars.
Food	Flying insects.
Range	Widespread in C and W Europe.
Similar species	Whiskered Bat.

NATTERER'S BAT *Myotis nattereri*

This medium-sized *Myotis* bat is light brownish above and whitish below with a pale muzzle and relatively long ears. The tail membrane has a characteristic fringe of hairs along the edge. It is active by night. In summer it roosts in tree holes or cracks in buildings and in winter it hibernates, on its own or in colonies, usually in caves or tunnels.

Size	42–55 mm, plus a tail of up to 47 mm, and a wingspan of up to 30 cm.
Habitat	Generally wooded areas with good roost sites.
Food	Flying insects and spiders.
Range	Widespread over most of Europe as far north as Britain, Ireland and S Scandinavia.
Similar species	Other *Myotis* bats.

GREATER MOUSE-EARED BAT *Myotis myotis*

One of Europe's largest bats, it is grey above and whitish below. The ears are large and mouse-like, and the face is almost hairless. During the breeding season females often form large nursery colonies and the single young is born in early summer and has greyer fur than the adult.

Size	67–79 mm, plus a tail of up to 60 mm, and a wingspan of up to 45 cm.
Habitat	Mainly open woodland, but also in towns, where it roosts in church towers and roof spaces.
Food	Insects and spiders.
Range	Widespread in C and S Europe. Extinct in British Isles and declining elsewhere.
Similar species	Other *Myotis* bats, but they are smaller.

COMMON NOCTULE *Nyctalus noctula*

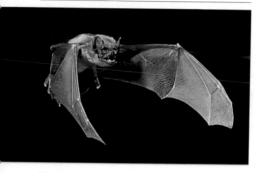

The Common Noctule is a large bat, weighing up to 40 g, with sleek reddish fur and long, narrow wings. It prefers woodland and roosts in tree holes; in winter it hibernates in trees, rock clefts and cracks in houses. It squeaks are often heard as it emerges just before sunset. It flies high and makes sudden twisting dives.

Size	60–80 mm, plus a tail of up to 60 mm, and a wingspan of up to 40 cm.
Habitat	Woodland, pasture and parkland.
Food	Large insects caught and eaten on the wing.
Range	Widespread across most of Europe except N Scandinavia, Scotland and Ireland.
Similar species	Leisler's Bat (opposite) and Greater Noctule, *N. lasiopterus*, are less common and widespread.

·LEISLER'S BAT *Nyctalus leisleri*

Similar to the Common Noctule (opposite), but smaller and noticeably darker; it does not fly as high or dive as steeply. During the summer it roosts mainly in tree holes, but occasionally in buildings, with breeding colonies of up to several hundred females. One litter is born each year with a single young in the west of its range, and twins in the east.

Size	48–68 mm, plus a tail of up to 45 mm, and a wingspan of up to 32 cm.
Habitat	Woodland.
Food	Moths, beetles and other flying insects.
Range	Fragmented across most of Europe, east to the Russian states and south to Greece and Bulgaria.
Similar species	Common Noctule and Greater Noctule, *N. lasiopterus*.

SEROTINE *Eptesicus serotinus*

This large, fairly heavily built bat has dark brown fur and rounded, blackish ears; its underparts are paler. The wings are broad and the flight distinctive – it hunts with a looping flight, often along hedges and edges of woodland. It usually emerges to feed before dark and flies high, rarely twisting and diving.

Size	62–82 mm, plus a tail of up to 59 mm, and a wingspan up to 38 cm.
Habitat	Woodland and parks, often near human habitation.
Food	Insects.
Range	Widespread and often abundant across Europe, as far north as S England and Wales.
Similar species	Northern Bat (opposite) and Parti-coloured Bat (p.40).

NORTHERN BAT *Eptesicus nilssoni*

Smaller than the Serotine (opposite), the Northern Bat has longer, less rounded ears. The fur is brown, tinged with yellow above giving it a glossy sheen, and paler below. It is fast flying and often hunts over the tops of trees or above water. The females gather in nursery colonies of up to 60, and have 1–2 young each year.

Size	45–64 mm, plus a tail of up to 50 mm, and a wingspan of up to 28 cm.
Habitat	Mainly open woodland; also around farms.
Food	Insects.
Range	Widely in Scandinavia (the only bat north of the Arctic Circle), south to N Romania.
Similar species	Serotine.

PARTI-COLOURED BAT *Vespertilio murinus*

This bat is striking: the hairs on the upperparts are dark brown with white tips giving it a 'frosted' appearance, which contrasts with the paler undersides. Its flight is fast and straight and it is known to migrate up to 900 km. Originally roosting in cliffs and rocky hillsides, more recently it has adapted to urban areas including tower blocks in cities.

Size	48–64 mm, plus a tail of up to 45 mm, and a wingspan of up to 31 cm.
Habitat	Woodland, farms, cliffs; also towns and cities.
Food	Insects.
Range	C and E Europe, north to S Scandinavia and south to Greece and Italy.
Similar species	Serotine (p.38) and Northern Bat (p.39).

COMMON PIPISTRELLE *Pipistrellus pipistrellus*

This is the most widespread (and smallest) of the 4 species of pipistrelles, which are Europe's smallest bats. Its colour is variable, but is generally brownish above and paler below. The ears and muzzle are dark and the short ears are rounded. In Eastern Europe roosts of up to 100,000 individuals have been found in caves.

Size	32–51 mm, plus a tail of up to 36 mm, and a wingspan up to 24 cm.
Habitat	Most habitats, except heavily built-up areas.
Food	A wide variety of small insects.
Range	Most of Europe except the extreme north.
Similar species	Other pipistrelles.

KUHL'S PIPISTRELLE *Pipistrellus kuhli*

Very similar to the Common Pipistrelle (p.41), but generally slightly paler. On close examination it has proportionally broader wings and a shorter thumb – but these characteristics cannot be seen in flight. During the breeding season the females gather in small nursery colonies, of around 20 individuals, and give birth to twins.

Size	40–47 mm, plus a tail of up to 34 mm, and a wingspan up to 24 cm.
Habitat	Mostly woodland.
Food	Insects and spiders.
Range	S Europe and W France.
Similar species	Savi's Pipistrelle, *P. savii*, and Nathusius's Pipistrelle, *P. nathusii*, also occur in Europe.

Brown Long-eared Bat *Plecotus auritus*

The ears of this bat are almost as long as the body and are joined together at the base by a membrane fold along the forehead. It usually emerges after sunset, and has a hovering flight as it hunts for food along the edges of woods. It rarely migrates and does not breed until 2 or 3 years old.

Size 42–55 mm, plus a tail of up to 55 mm, and a wingspan of up to 28.5 cm.
Habitat Woodland and gardens.
Food Insects and spiders; moths in summer.
Range Throughout most of Europe.
Similar species Grey Long-eared Bat (p.44).

GREY LONG-EARED BAT *Plecotus austriacus*

A very similar bat to the Brown Long-eared Bat (p.43), with ears almost as long as the body. The tragus (inner ear lobe) is grey, not translucent, as in the Brown Long-eared Bat. It usually emerges after sunset, and has a hovering flight as it hunts for food along the edges of woods, over open fields and around street lights. It was not properly identified as a separate species until the 1960s.

Size	42–58 mm, plus a tail of up to 55 mm, and a wingspan of up to 30 cm.
Habitat	Woodland and gardens.
Food	Insects and spiders; moths in summer.
Range	Across most of S Europe; rare in S England.
Similar species	Brown Long-eared Bat.

BARBASTELLE BAT *Barbastella barbastellus*

This medium-sized bat is almost black on the back and sides, and only slightly paler below; the fur has a 'frosted' appearance. The ears, while quite short, are very large and meet over the head; the face has a characteristic wrinkled appearance. It hibernates in caves, tunnels and trees, and a single young is born in summer.

Size	45–58 mm, plus a tail of up to 50 mm, and a wingspan of up to 29 cm.
Habitat	Woodland, particularly mountainous areas.
Food	Insects.
Range	Most of Europe, north to S England and Scandinavia.
Similar species	None.

SCHREIBER'S BAT *Miniopterus schreibersi*

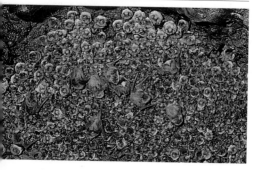

This bat has a short muzzle and a domed head which is covered with short, erect soft fur, different in texture from that on its back. The wings are long and narrow, and it is fast-flying. It is highly colonial and often mixes with colonies of *Myotis* bats, roosting in caves and buildings. It migrates in winter.

Size	48–62 mm, plus a tail of up to 64 mm, and a wingspan of up to 34.2 cm.
Habitat	Prefers open countryside in limestone areas.
Food	Insects.
Range	Confined to S & E Europe; numbers declining.
Similar species	None.

FREE-TAILED BAT *Tadarida teniotis*

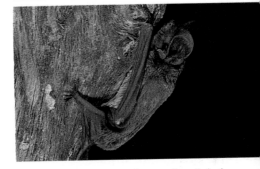

This is the largest European bat, very heavily built and weighing up to 50 g. The distinctive ears point forwards and it has a wrinkled face. Only half the long tail is covered by the wing membrane, making it visible in flight. It has swallow-like wings and flies high with a very fast flight. The single young is born each year in summer.

Size	80–92 mm, plus a tail of up to 57 mm, and a wingspan of up to 44 cm.
Habitat	Hilly country, cliffs and gorges.
Food	Insects.
Range	Confined to Mediterranean regions.
Similar species	None.

RABBITS AND HARES

Rabbits and hares (lagomorphs) are rather similar to rodents, and were at one time classified with them. The most important difference is in the teeth – lagomorphs have tiny secondary incisors behind the upper incisors. The European species differ from the rodents by having long ears, relatively long hind legs, and short fluffy tails. The European Rabbit is colonial and lives in extensive colonies known as warrens; the young are born blind and helpless. It is the ancestor of the domestic rabbit, which now occurs in a wide range of colours, as well as lop-eared varieties, angoras (with long fur) and rex (with short velvety fur). The hares are generally less gregarious, though some species will form herds during winter months. Hares give birth to fully furred young, with their eyes open. Rabbits and hares have been important game animals over most of Europe.

In spring, groups of Brown Hares can be seen 'boxing', part of their courtship behaviour

RABBIT *Oryctolagus cuniculus*

Originally from north-west Africa, Spain and Portugal, the Rabbit was introduced and has spread through most of Europe. Although they are usually brown, black individuals are not uncommon. They are mainly active at dusk and dawn and live colonially, having 2 or 3 litters a year of 2–8 young. When alarmed they stamp their hind feet as a warning.

Size	Up to 55 cm, plus a short tail.
Habitat	Grassland, meadows and scrub.
Food	Grass, leaves and crops.
Range	Widespread throughout most of W Europe.
Similar	Hares (pp.52 & 53) are larger and not colonial.
species	Cottontail (opposite) does not burrow.

COTTONTAIL *Sylvilagus floridanus*

The Cottontail is very similar to the Rabbit (opposite), but is smaller and has shorter, black-tipped ears. It was introduced into Europe from the USA and its range is spreading; it may be displacing the native European species. Unlike the European Rabbit it does not excavate burrows, but gives birth to 3–4 young in a nest above ground.

Size	Up to 43 cm, plus a tail of up to 65 mm.
Habitat	Agricultural land, scrub and thickets.
Food	Grasses and vegetation.
Range	Introduced into France and N Italy.
Similar species	Rabbit.

BROWN HARE *Lepus europaeus*

Hares are sandy brown above, lighter below and have long, black-tipped ears; the tail has a black top. Usually solitary, they do not dig burrows, but scrape a depression (form) in the ground. They can run at a great speed and frequently twist and change direction in mid-air. The 1–5 young (leverets) are born fully furred and are active within a few hours.

Size	Up to 70 cm, plus a tail of up to 11 cm.
Habitat	Open woodland and grassland.
Food	Grasses, shoots, twigs and leaves.
Range	Across Europe, except N Scotland, Eire, N Scandinavia and much of Spain and Portugal.
Similar species	Mountain Hare (opposite) and Spanish Hare, *L. castroviejoi*.

Mountain Hare *Lepus timidus*

Distinguished from the Brown Hare (opposite) by its shorter ears and an all-white tail; most populations turn white in winter, except for the black ear-tips. However, in Ireland (and elsewhere at lower altitudes) the summer coat is brighter and only fades slightly in winter. It has 2 or 3 litters a year of 2–5 young, which are active soon after birth.

Size	Up to 65 cm, plus a tail of up to 8 cm.
Habitat	Open tundra, heathland, farmland and mountains.
Food	Grasses, heather, sedges and twigs.
Range	Scandinavia, Finland and the E Russian states; also Scotland, Ireland, the Faeroes, Alps and Pyrenees.
Similar species	Brown Hare, but ranges rarely overlap.

RODENTS

Rodents are the most numerous group of mammals in the world – there are more species of rodent than in any other group, and there are more individuals. They are also among the most serious pests, causing millions of pounds worth of damage to man's crops and property. The rodents include rats, mice, squirrels, beavers, dormice and several other families. They all have almost identical teeth, consisting of a pair of incisors on the upper and lower jaws, a gap (the diastema) and a row of grinders. The incisors are usually pigmented yellowish or bright orange. Most rodents are herbivores, feeding on leaves, seeds, nuts and other vegetable matter, but many will also feed on insects, grubs and even carrion. Their external appearance is more varied – some have long tails, others almost no tail. Some are aquatic, others are arboreal (live in trees). Although most are relatively dull coloured – usually brown or grey – a few have quite distinctive markings. Most give birth to naked, blind and helpless young, with sometimes as many as 12 or more in a litter.

Brown Rats have large litters and a short gestation period, so populations can build up to plague proportions very quickly

RED SQUIRREL *Sciurus vulgaris*

The Red Squirrel is usually reddish-brown above and whitish below, but black individuals are not uncommon. In summer it has pointed ear tufts and the tail often bleaches to a pale cream. It lives in trees, and builds a bulky nest (drey) in tree forks or in hollow trees. The 3–7 young are born blind and helpless.

Size	18–27 cm, plus a tail of up to 20 cm.
Habitat	Woodland, parkland and forest.
Food	Shoots, nuts, fruits and bark.
Range	Widespread over most of Europe, except parts of Spain and Portugal and much of England.
Similar species	Persian Squirrel, *S. anomalus*, on the island of Lesbos, Greece.

GREY SQUIRREL *Sciurus carolinensis*

Native to North America, the Grey Squirrel was introduced into Britain at the end of the 19th century. It is larger than the Red Squirrel (opposite), lacks the ear tufts, and is more adaptable – it often lives in close proximity to humans, raiding bird tables etc. The 2 litters a year have 1–7 young each.

Size	Up to 30 cm, plus a tail of up to 24 cm.
Habitat	Woodland, parkland, and gardens.
Food	Nuts, berries, roots and shoots; also insects and eggs.
Range	Widespread in England and Wales, with an increasing range.
Similar species	Unlikely to be confused with the Red Squirrel.

SIBERIAN CHIPMUNK *Tamias sibiricus*

Originating from Siberia, this small, bushy-tailed squirrel has five clearly defined dark stripes down the back and sides. It is active by day, showing much agility as it leaps from branch to branch, usually in low trees. It has cheek pouches for carrying and storing food, which it hoards for use during the winter, when it is less active.

Size	15–22 cm, plus a tail of up to 24 cm.
Habitat	Forested areas with thick undergrowth.
Food	Nuts, seeds, fruit and roots.
Range	E Finland and Russian states, with scattered, introduced populations in France, Germany, Netherlands and Austria.
Similar species	Chipmunk, *T. striatus*, has also been introduced.

EUROPEAN SOUSLIK *Spermophilus citellus*

Sousliks have large eyes, short ears and a furry tail, and this species is buff-brown, with no distinct markings. It lives in colonies and sits upright in a 'begging' position as it keeps watch for danger. It is active by day, and excavates extensive underground tunnels, in which it breeds, stores food, and hibernates.

Size	Up to 22 cm, plus a tail of up to 4.5 cm.
Habitat	Open steppes and arable land.
Food	Seeds, grain and herbage, which it stores underground.
Range	Widespread in E Europe.
Similar species	Spotted Souslik, *S. suslicus*, which has white spots on the back.

ALPINE MARMOT *Marmota marmota*

The Alpine Marmot is a heavily built ground squirrel with small ears and a short, bushy tail. It is extremely sociable and can often be seen playing on sunny mornings, watched over by a 'guard' who gives a sharp whistle to warn of danger. It produces one litter a year of 2–6 young, born blind and helpless.

Size	40–60 cm, plus a tail of up to 20 cm.
Habitat	Mountain meadows.
Food	Grasses and herbage; carries dry grass to its burrow for bedding.
Range	The Alps and Tatra Mountains; reintroduced elsewhere.
Similar species	None.

BEAVER *Castor fiber*

The largest rodent in Europe, the Beaver has a blunt muzzle and a flattened, hairless tail. It builds extensive 'lodges' and dams – except populations on the Rhine river in France, which live in burrows instead. It swims well and can stay submerged for up to 15 minutes. Beavers mate for life, and have a single litter a year of 2–6 young.

Size	75–100 cm, plus a tail of up to 40 cm.
Habitat	Rivers, lakes and swamps, with trees.
Food	Bark, shoots, aquatic plants and other vegetation.
Range	A few isolated colonies on the Rhine, the Elbe (Poland), in Scandinavia and Russia. Also many reintroductions, some of American Beaver, *C. canadensis*.
Similar species	Coypu, *Myocastor coypus*, and Musk Rat (p.76).

61

PORCUPINE *Hystrix cristata*

A very large rodent easily recognised by its long black and white quills, which can often be found in and around its dens. It lives in small groups, making dens in burrows or among rocks. It feeds on roots and vegetables and often does considerable damage to gardens and crops. When alarmed it rattles its quills, and reverses towards the intruder.

Size Up to about 70 cm, plus a short tail.

Habitat Rocky hillsides, olive groves, open woodland.

Food A wide range of vegetable foods.

Range A North African species, introduced into Sicily and mainland Italy.

Similar species Only likely to be confused with Hedgehog (p.16), which is much smaller.

GARDEN DORMOUSE *Eliomys quercinus*

The Garden Dormouse can be identified by its tail (which has a flattened, black and white tuft at the tip), its black facial mask and large ears. Its nest is built in a cleft in a wall or among rocks, often using an old bird's nest as a base. It is active by night, and has 1–2 litters a year, each of 2–9 young.

Size	10–18 cm, plus a tail of up to 13 cm.
Habitat	Woodland, scrub, orchards, parks and gardens.
Food	Invertebrates, nestling birds, eggs and small mammals. In autumn, fruit, berries, and seeds.
Range	Across most of Europe, except the British Isles, Iceland and Scandinavia.
Similar species	Other dormice.

EDIBLE DORMOUSE *Glis glis*

Also known as the Fat Dormouse, this is the largest of the dormice. It is grey, except for dark rings around the eyes, and its tail is long and bushy. Before hibernation it gorges on food and becomes very fat; it is so-called because the Romans fattened them to eat. The 2–7 young are born in early summer and have been known to live for 9 years.

Size	12–20 cm, plus a tail of up to 19 cm.
Habitat	Deciduous woodland with dense undergrowth.
Food	Buds, bark, shoots, fruit; also insects and birds' eggs.
Range	Most of Europe, except much of Spain, Portugal and Scandinavia. Introduced into England.
Similar species	Grey Squirrel (p.57), which is larger.

HAZEL DORMOUSE *Muscardinus avellenarius*

In size the Hazel Dormouse resembles a large mouse, although it is the smallest of the dormice. The fur is bright orange-brown on top and whitish below, and the tail is also furred, giving it a bushy appearance. It is an agile climber, with prehensile feet, and is active at night. The nest is made from stripped bark and it has 1–2 litters a year, each of 2–6 young.

Size	6–8.5 cm, plus a tail of up to 8 cm.
Habitat	Woodland with shrubbery; likes honeysuckle.
Food	Nuts, seeds, berries and fruit; also insects and occasionally eggs.
Range	Across most of Europe, except N Spain, Portugal and Ireland.
Similar species	Harvest Mouse (p.81) is smaller with a naked tail.

COMMON HAMSTER *Cricetus cricetus*

The Hamster is a burrowing rodent with a plump, furry body and a short, haired tail. Its colour varies: the upperparts are brown with a variety of paler patches, and the underparts are blackish. It lives in colonies in burrows, with chambers for storing food, eating and sleeping, and hibernates in a nest made of leaves or grasses. Up to 3 litters are born a year, each of 3–15 young.

Size	22–34 cm, plus a tail of up to 6 cm.
Habitat	Steppes, farmland and grassland.
Food	Grain, seeds and roots; also invertebrates.
Range	E Europe, also scattered populations west to Belgium and N France.
Similar species	Romanian Hamster, *Mesocricetus newtoni*, but range does not overlap.

NORWAY LEMMING *Lemmus lemmus*

The bold golden and black markings on the back make this lemming very distinctive; the underside is paler. In the summer it burrows extensively, in winter it makes its nest in tunnels beneath the snow. The Norway Lemming populations fluctuate dramatically, and they migrate en masse. Four litters or more are born a year, of 2–13 young, which can be mature when 3 weeks old.

Size	13–15 cm, plus a tail of up to 2 cm.
Habitat	Mountain tundra.
Food	Grasses, sedges, mosses and shrubs.
Range	Norway, Sweden, Finland and Arctic Scandinavia.
Similar species	Unlikely to be confused with any other species.

BANK VOLE *Clethrionomys glareolus*

The Bank Vole is rather mouse-like, but has a blunter nose, more prominent ears and a shorter tail. The fur is reddish-brown, and greyer on the undersides. Active day and night, it makes shallow burrows under grass and leaves, and also climbs among shrubbery. It does not hibernate, and females have up to 4 litters a year, of 3–6 young.

Size	8–12 cm, plus a tail of up to 65 mm.
Habitat	Mostly wooded habitats, hedgerows and gardens.
Food	A wide variety of vegetable matter including roots, nuts and fungi; occasionally insects and molluscs.
Range	Across Europe, except the extreme north and south. Introduced into Ireland.
Similar species	Other voles.

FIELD VOLE *Microtus agrestis*

The Field, or Short-tailed, Vole differs from the Common Vole (p.70) in having a longer, shaggier coat. The tail is darker above than below, and the ears slightly hairy. Active by day and night, it tunnels extensively just below ground level and makes its nest of finely shredded grass. Six litters are born a year, each of 2–12 young.

Size	9–14 cm, plus a tail of up to 52 mm.
Habitat	Mostly grassy habitats.
Food	Grass and vegetable matter; occasionally insects.
Range	From N Portugal to E Europe, and north to Great Britain and the Arctic Circle. Absent from much of S Europe and Ireland.
Similar species	Other *Microtus* voles.

COMMON VOLE *Microtus arvalis*

Very similar to the Field Vole (p.69), but on close inspection the ears are less hairy; also it is a generally lighter greyish-brown. It burrows deeper than other voles and can therefore survive in areas where there is less ground cover, such as grazed pastures. It is mainly active at night. Up to 6 litters are born a year, each of up to 12 young.

Size	8–13 cm, plus a tail of up to 50 mm.
Habitat	Variety of grassland, including pasture.
Food	Vegetable matter, berries and some insects.
Range	Widespread in mainland Europe from France and Spain to Russia. Introduced into the Orkney islands.
Similar species	Other *Microtus* voles.

BALKAN SNOW VOLE *Dinaromys bogdanovi*

Also known as Martino's Snow Vole, this distinctive, long-tailed vole has soft, pale grey Chinchilla-like fur. Active by night, it makes extensive burrows, often around the base of rocks, and usually nests under stones or in a crack in rocks, but sometimes actually in the snow. Two litters are born a year, of only 2–3 young in each.

Size	10–15.2 cm, plus a tail of up to 11 cm.
Habitat	Rocky areas above the tree line.
Food	Grasses, roots and other vegetation.
Range	Confined to the west of the former Yugoslavia and Albania.
Similar species	Snow Vole (p.72) and other *Microtus* voles, but ranges rarely overlap.

Snow Vole *Microtus nivalis*

A large vole, with longish grey or greyish-brown fur, a long whitish tail, and prominent whiskers. Active mainly by day, though also at night, it does not tunnel, but makes its runs among rocks and often basks in the sun. It does not hibernate, but stores food. Two litters are born a year, each of 1–5 young.

Size	8.5–14 cm, plus a tail of up to 75 mm.
Habitat	Mountain meadows and grassland mainly above the tree line; in France at lower altitudes.
Food	Shoots, herbs, grasses, nuts and berries.
Range	Isolated populations in many mountains in C and S Europe.
Similar species	Balkan Snow Vole (p.71).

COMMON PINE VOLE *Pitymys subterraneus*

This is the most widespread and best known of the pine voles. It is greyish with slightly paler underparts. It is active by day and night, but more during the day, though it excavates extensive tunnels and spends most of its time underground. There are 2–3 litters born a year, each with 2–4 young.

Size	8–10.2 cm, plus a tail of up to 40 mm.
Habitat	Woodland and well-vegetated areas.
Food	Grasses, seeds, bulbs and roots.
Range	From France eastwards to Russia.
Similar species	There at least 7 other species of pine voles in Europe.

Northern Water Vole *Arvicola terrestris*

This large vole varies in colour, but is usually dark brown. Although mainly found in wetlands, it can occur far from water. It is active by day and night, and is often easily visible. When burrowing it makes 'tumps' of soil, similar to those of moles. The 3–4 litters a year each have up to 6 young.

Size	12–19 cm, plus a tail of up to 10 cm.
Habitat	Meadows, fields, wetlands and riversides.
Food	Mostly vegetation matter; also fish and carrion.
Range	Most of Europe except SW France, Spain, Portugal and Ireland.
Similar species	Southern Water Vole (opposite).

SOUTHERN WATER VOLE *Arvicola sapidus*

A large vole very similar to the Northern Water Vole (opposite), but generally larger and darker, and with a proportionally longer tail. Like the Northern Water Vole it is active by day and night, and is often easily visible. It is very rarely seen away from water.

Size	17–20 cm, plus a tail of up to 13 cm.
Habitat	Wet meadows, lakes, canals and riversides.
Food	Mostly vegetation matter; also fish and carrion.
Range	W France, Spain, Portugal.
Similar species	Northern Water Vole.

Musk Rat *Ondatra zibethicus*

The largest species of vole, with dense, rich-brown fur. Originally from North America, it was introduced into European fur farms and escapees colonised many European countries including Britain, where it was exterminated in 1937. It swims well (having webbed hind feet) and builds nests in aquatic vegetation. It has 1–4 litters a year, of 5–10 young.

Size 25–40 cm, plus a tail of up to 25 cm.

Habitat Wetlands, lakes and slow-moving rivers.

Food Aquatic plants and most vegetation, some animal matter; also raids food crops.

Range France, east to Russia.

Similar species Coypu, *Myocastor coypus*, and Beaver (p.61), which are both larger. Also Otter (p.104).

BLACK RAT *Rattus rattus*

Also known as the Ship or House Rat, it has largely been displaced by the Brown Rat (p.78), particularly in Britain and Scandinavia. Its colour varies, although it is usually blackish, with a long, bald tail. The ears are large and the muzzle rather pointed. It is usually active by night. The 3–5 litters a year each have up to 16 young.

Size	16–24 cm, plus a tail of up to 26 cm.
Habitat	Wide variety, usually close to man.
Food	They are opportunistic, eating almost anything.
Range	Widespread in C and S Europe; scattered populations in British Isles and N Europe.
Similar species	Brown Rat is larger.

BROWN RAT *Rattus norvegicus*

The Brown Rat is usually brown above and greyer below, but there are wide variations. It makes extensive burrows, but is as much at home in water as on land, and may be confused with water voles when swimming. It is one of the most serious mammal pests causing much damage, but it is also important prey for many other animals. It has up to 5 litters a year, of 7–15 young.

Size	20–28 cm, plus a tail of up to 23 cm.
Habitat	Mainly around human settlements.
Food	Almost anything.
Range	Introduced by man from Asia, occurs throughout Europe, including islands.
Similar species	Water voles (pp.74 & 75) and Black Rat (p.77).

WOOD MOUSE *Apodemus sylvaticus*

The commonest mouse throughout much of Europe and an important prey for many mammals and birds. The upperparts are sandy-brown, and the underside is silvery-white. It is extremely agile and mainly active at night. It does not hibernate, and in milder winters when food supplies are good it will breed late into autumn. It has up to 4 litters a year, of 3–9 young.

Size	7.5–11 cm, plus a tail of up to 11 cm.
Habitat	Woodland, also gardens and hedgerows.
Food	Seeds, fruit, plants and invertebrates.
Range	Widespread across most of Europe, including islands, except far north.
Similar species	Yellow-necked Mouse (p.80).

79

YELLOW-NECKED MOUSE *Apodemus flavicollis*

Similar to the Wood Mouse (p.79), but slightly larger, it has lighter, richer-brown fur above, and is paler underneath. There is always a yellowish-brown band of fur on the throat. It burrows less than the Wood Mouse and often enters houses. Up to 3 litters are born each year, of 2–9 young.

Size 8–13 cm, plus a tail of up to 13 cm.

Habitat Woodland, orchards, gardens and hedgerows.

Food Seeds, berries and fruits, and some insects.

Range Mainly E and C Europe, north to Scandinavia and Finland, west to France and N Spain. Also S England and Wales.

Similar species Wood Mouse, which lacks the chest band.

HARVEST MOUSE *Micromys minutus*

The smallest European rodent. It is rich reddish above and whitish below, with very small ears. It is extremely agile, using its partially prehensile tail to move quickly through tall vegetation. The nest is a spherical ball of woven grasses, usually attached to the stems of growing grasses. It has several litters a year, of up to 6 young.

Size	50–80 mm, plus a tail of up to 75 mm.
Habitat	Meadows, hedgerows, reedbeds and agricultural land.
Food	Seeds, berries, shoots and buds; also insects.
Range	Widespread in Europe from NW Spain to S Britain, Denmark and S Finland, and east to the Russian states, Greece and Bulgaria. Absent from higher altitudes and most of the Mediterranean.
Similar species	Birch Mice and House Mice. A recently described species of Harvest Mouse, which is larger with a longer tail, occurs in a small area in Romania.

WESTERN HOUSE MOUSE *Mus domesticus*

Brownish-grey above and paler below, the House Mouse is common around human habitations in both rural and urban areas. Mainly active at night, it is an agile climber and it runs in straight lines. Up to 10 litters are born each year, of up to 9 naked and helpless young.

Size	75–95 mm, plus a tail of up to 95 mm.
Habitat	Usually associated with human habitation.
Food	Seeds and grain; scavenges on human waste.
Range	Common across W Europe, as far east as Denmark and the Adriatic.
Similar species	Eastern House Mouse, *M. musculus*, is slightly larger, with a paler belly; ranges rarely overlap. Alpine House Mouse *M. poschiavinus*, occurs in S Switzerland and the Italian Alps.

ALGERIAN HOUSE MOUSE *Mus spretus*

This mouse is similar to the Western and Eastern House Mouse (p.82), but smaller, often browner above and whitish below, with a shorter tail. Unlike the House Mouse it does not always live in association with man, and often builds its nest of grasses and leaves in woodland areas. It is active day and night, and up to 10 litters are born a year, of up to 9 young.

Size	67–88 mm, plus a tail of up to 74 mm.
Habitat	Gardens, woodland, scrub and agricultural land.
Food	Seeds, grain and a wide variety of vegetable matter.
Range	Throughout Spain, Portugal and Mediterranean France.
Similar species	Other small mice.

SPINY MOUSE *Acomys cahirinus*

This mouse is similar in size and general appearance to the Wood Mouse (p.79), but the fur has stiff, spiny hairs on the back. The tail is frequently broken, occurring when it is handled or attacked, often leaving a short stump. It is active by day and night, and does not hibernate. Several litters are born each year, of 1–5 young.

Size	9–12.5 cm, plus a tail of up to 12 cm.
Habitat	Dry, often rocky areas, also gardens.
Food	Seeds, and some invertebrates.
Range	In Europe, it is only found on Crete.
Similar species	Wood mice, but no other mouse has spiny fur.

NORTHERN BIRCH MOUSE *Sicista betulina*

The yellowish-brown fur of this mouse has a conspicuous dark stripe running from the head to the base of the long, partially prehensile, tail. It is active by night, spending the daytime in burrows and foraging at night; its high-pitched whistle is distinctive. A single litter of 2–11 young is born in the summer.

Size	50–78 mm, plus a tail of up to 10.5 cm.
Habitat	Dense vegetation in woodland and meadows.
Food	Small insects with some seeds and berries.
Range	Patchy distribution from Scandinavia, Finland and W Russia, south through Germany, Poland, Czech Republic and Romania.
Similar species	Southern Birch Mouse, *S. subtilis*, is greyer with a shorter tail. Harvest Mouse (p.81) is unstriped.

PRIMATES

The only primate that is native to Europe is the human species, *Homo sapiens*. The Barbary Ape was introduced from North Africa into Gibraltar where, although it lives in the wild, the population is artificially maintained. The primates consist of lemurs, bush babies, monkeys and true apes. The latter are the tailless apes – the gorillas, Orang-Utan, chimpanzees and humans. The Barbary Ape is not a true ape, but an Old World Monkey, a macaque, although it lacks a tail. Like many other monkeys they have a well-developed social structure.

BARBARY APE *Macaca sylvanus*

The only primate found in Europe (apart from humans), it was introduced into Gibraltar from North Africa. In common with most monkeys, its muzzle is short, the eyes relatively large and the ears short; it does not have a tail. One young is born every other year, and they have been known to live for over 15 years.

Size	60–70 cm, with no tail.
Habitat	Rocky hillsides, with scrub.
Food	Mainly vegetation, but they are fed regularly to discourage them going nearer to the town.
Range	Only on the Rock of Gibraltar, and numbering under 50. Have adapted to living close to man.
Similar species	None in Europe.

CARNIVORES

Carnivores are extremely diverse in appearance ranging from the mouse-sized Weasel to the Polar Bear. They are mostly predators, with teeth adapted for killing their prey, and for tearing meat; in particular, most have well-developed canine teeth. They also have thick fur, which in several species has led to them being extensively hunted, and some are bred on fur farms. Many species have been persecuted because of their predation on livestock, and most of the larger species are extinct over much of Europe, only surviving in the more remote areas or in parks and reserves. The young of carnivores are usually born blind and helpless, and are often very playful while growing up, staying with the mother while they learn to hunt. Although carnivores are mostly predators, several species take a large proportion of invertebrate food, and they may also feed on fruits and carrion (i.e. they may be omnivorous, meaning they feed on both animals and plants).

Because they have been persecuted for so long they are generally shy and their presence is often only detected by their footprints, remains of prey and other signs.

Like most carnivores, Red Fox young are very playful

POLAR BEAR *Ursus maritimus*

The largest of the bears, the Polar Bear can weigh up to 750 kg. It is mainly aquatic, living among ice floes, and is an exceptionally strong swimmer. It spends the winter in a den, and the single young (or twins) is tiny at birth (no bigger than a rabbit) and does not leave the den for 4 months. It has lived to over 30 years in captivity.

Size	1.6–2.5 m, plus a tail of up to 10 cm.
Habitat	Floating ice and polar regions.
Food	Seals, walruses, whale calves and fishes; also carrion and vegetable matter, including lichens and moss.
Range	Around the North Pole, in Arctic Canada, Alaska and the Russian states, Scandinavia and Greenland.
Similar species	None.

BROWN BEAR *Ursus arctos*

The Brown Bear once occurred over most of the northern hemisphere, but is now reduced to isolated populations. It varies from pale brown to black. It is solitary, mainly active by night, and hibernates in dens. The young (usually twins, but sometimes up to 6) are looked after by their mother until the following year.

Size	Up to 2 m, with no tail.
Habitat	Forest, woodland and tundra.
Food	A variety of plants, berries, fruit and fungus; also carrion, fish, insects, honey; occasionally livestock.
Range	More remote mountains of Spain, Italy, France, Scandinavia and E Europe.
Similar species	None.

WOLF *Canis lupus*

The Wolf is a powerful and intelligent animal. In the north of its range it tends to be more heavily built and more thickly furred. It lives in family groups, and the young (up to 5 in a litter) stay with the parents for up to a year; the male brings food for his mate and cubs. Although predators of livestock, Wolves do not attack humans.

Size	1–1.6 m, plus a tail of up to 50 cm.
Habitat	Open woodland and tundra, also forest.
Food	Mostly mammals, up to the size of deer; also fruit.
Range	Only small isolated populations survive, in Norway, Sweden, Italy, Spain and E Europe.
Similar species	Domestic dogs, particularly Alsatians (German Shepherds) and, in SE Europe, Jackal (opposite).

JACKAL *Canis aureus*

A slender, long-legged dog, much lighter in build than the Wolf (opposite), and more reddish in colour. Mainly active at night, it generally hunts alone, but will occasionally form small packs. It is extremely vocal, particularly at dusk, when it makes a range of howlings and barks, often in chorus. The single annual litter is usually born in a burrow, and has 3–9 cubs.

Size	71–85 cm, plus a tail of up to 30 cm.
Habitat	Grassland and cultivated land, usually around human settlements.
Food	Rodents, birds and carrion; frequently scavenges. Will raid domestic livestock.
Range	SE Europe from NE Italy and Austria southwards.
Similar species	Domestic dogs, and Wolves.

RED FOX *Vulpes vulpes*

Rich brownish-red above and white below, the Red Fox is dog-like in appearance with pointed ears, a narrow muzzle and a bushy, white-tipped tail. The back of the ears and paws are often blackish. It is mainly active at night and does not hibernate. The single annual litter has 3–8 cubs, which are born in an underground earth.

Size	60–90 cm, plus a tail of up to 60 cm.
Habitat	Almost all habitats providing cover. Has adapted well to urban areas.
Food	Mainly small mammals; also fruit and poultry.
Range	Widespread throughout Europe.
Similar species	Domestic dogs, Jackal (p.93) and Arctic Fox (opposite).

ARCTIC FOX *Alopex lagopus*

The Arctic Fox has a short muzzle and rounded ears, and occurs in two distinct colour phases: some animals are pure white in winter and brownish in summer, others are bluish-grey in winter and darker grey in summer. It is active by day and night and makes extensive burrows. Up to 2 litters are born each year, of up to 21 young (more usually 7–10).

Size	50–85 cm, plus a tail of up to 55 cm.
Habitat	Tundra and forest.
Food	Small mammals, birds and fruit; they also scavenge.
Range	Widespread in the Arctic, also on many northern islands including Iceland.
Similar species	Red Fox (opposite) and small domestic dogs.

RACCOON DOG *Nyctereutes procyonoides*

About the size of the Red Fox (p.94), the Raccoon Dog was introduced into Europe from the Far East. It was bred on fur farms in the then USSR and escaped animals became established. It has a shaggy coat and a short bob-tail, with a raccoon-like face mask. It has 1 litter a year, of 5–8 (sometimes up to 19) blind and helpless young.

Size	50–80 cm, plus a tail of up to 26 cm.
Habitat	Variable, usually in wooded areas, near water.
Food	Rodents, amphibians, fruit and vegetable matter.
Range	From E France and Sweden, eastwards; still spreading.
Similar species	Raccoon (p.107).

STOAT *Mustela erminea*

The Stoat's fur is reddish-brown above and creamy-white below; the tail is black-tipped. In the northern parts of its range it turns white in winter, except for the black-tipped tail. It is active by day and night, and makes a variety of squeaking and hissing noises as it hunts. One litter is born each year, of up to 12 helpless young.

Size	17.5–30 cm, plus a tail of up to 14 cm.
Habitat	Wide variety, usually with woodland.
Food	Small mammals; also birds and eggs.
Range	Across most of Europe, except the Mediterranean.
Similar species	Weasel (p.98) is smaller and lacks the black tail tip.

WEASEL *Mustela nivalis*

This is the smallest European carnivore, which is very variable in size. It differs from the Stoat (p.97) in having a shorter tail without the black tip. It hunts on its own, by day or night, frequently standing on its hind legs to look around. The 1–2 litters a year each have 4–6 young (can be up to 12), which are born with white fur.

Size	11–26 cm, plus a tail of up to 87 mm.
Habitat	Wide variety, usually with woodland.
Food	Small mammals, mostly voles and mice.
Range	Across Europe, except Ireland, Iceland and a few other islands.
Similar species	Stoat.

AMERICAN MINK *Mustela vison*

Larger than the European Mink, the American Mink was introduced into European fur farms. It is now widespread in the wild as a result of escapes, and considered a pest in many areas. Generally lighter in colour than the European species, it is very variable and has less white on its muzzle. The single litter (of up to 6) is born in early summer.

Size	31–45 cm, plus a tail of up to 25 cm.
Habitat	Wide variety, usually near water.
Food	Wide variety, including fish, mammals, amphibians, invertebrates and birds.
Range	Widespread in Scandinavia and east to the Russian states; also Great Britain.
Similar species	Otter (p.104). European Mink, *M. lutreola*, is less widespread.

WESTERN POLECAT *Mustela putorius*

The Polecat is similar in size, and closely related, to the domestic ferret. It has a characteristic facial mask, long neck, small head and short legs. The creamy-yellow underfur shows through the longer, dark brown guard hairs. It is mainly active by night and is very vocal, making a variety of hissing and growling noises. One litter of 2–12 young is born each year.

Size	34–47 cm, plus a tail of up to 19 cm.
Habitat	Mainly woodland, often close to human habitation.
Food	Small mammals, birds and invertebrates.
Range	Occurs in Wales, but extinct across most of Great Britain. Widespread across most of rest of Europe.
Similar species	Domestic ferret. Steppe Polecat, *M. eversmanni*, and Marbled Polecat, *Vormela peregusna*, are both paler.

PINE MARTEN *Martes martes*

The Pine Marten is rich brown in colour, except for its irregularly shaped yellowish throat patch; the tail is long and bushy. Although generally active by night, it often emerges at dusk and dawn. It is an agile climber, and on land runs with a bounding gait. The single litter of 2–7 (usually 3) is born in spring, and the young are covered with pale fur.

Size	35–58 cm, plus a tail of up to 28 cm.
Habitat	Woodland and forest.
Food	Birds and small mammals; also berries and fruit.
Range	Most of Europe, except much of England, Spain, Portugal and Greece. Also on some islands.
Similar species	Beech Marten (p.102).

BEECH MARTEN *Martes foina*

Similar in size and colour to the Pine Marten (p.101), the Beech Marten has a white (rather than yellow) throat patch. Also known as the Stone Marten it is often found in arid, rocky areas where it excavates short burrows. It is mainly active morning and evening, but will emerge during the day. The single litter of 1–8 young is born in spring.

Size	44–54 cm, plus a tail of up to 32 cm.
Habitat	Woodland, scrub and rocky hillsides.
Food	Mainly small mammals and birds.
Range	Widespread across most of Europe, except British Isles and N Scandinavia.
Similar species	Pine Marten.

WOLVERINE *Gulo gulo*

The largest member of the weasel family, the Wolverine most resembles a small bear. The fur is long and dark brown with a paler stripe along the flanks. It does not hibernate and is active day and night. One litter of 2–3 young, born helpless but covered in white fur, is born in a den in late winter or spring.

Size	70–86 cm, plus a tail of up to 25 cm.
Habitat	Forest and tundra.
Food	Omnivorous, preys on animals up to the size of Reindeer.
Range	Much restricted: Arctic Scandinavia and Russia. Once occurred south to Germany.
Similar species	Brown Bear (p.91) is much larger; Pine Marten (p.101) is much smaller.

OTTER *Lutra lutra*

The Otter's glossy fur is water-resistant, the body streamlined and the feet webbed, equipping it for its aquatic life. Normally active by night and shy, it makes a variety of whistles and squeaks. It nests in a burrow (holt), usually among riverside tree roots, and has 1 litter a year of 1–5 young, which, although furred, are helpless and blind at birth.

Size	Up to 84 cm, plus a tail of up to 47 cm.
Habitat	Wetlands, rivers and coastal areas.
Food	Mainly fish, and aquatic animals including frogs.
Range	Rare or extinct over most of its former range, now only in Scotland, Ireland and Scandinavia. Small numbers re-introduced to Great Britain.
Similar species	Often confused with American Mink (p.99); also Coypu, *Myocastor coypus*, and Musk Rat (p.76).

BADGER *Meles meles*

The Badger has a heavily built body with a long snout, the fur is grey above, black below and the face is striped black and white. It lives in a burrow (sett) which has many chambers and several entrances. Although it does not hibernate, it stays in its sett during cold weather. The single litter of 1–5 young is born in winter or early spring.

Size	67–87 cm, plus a tail of up to 19 cm.
Habitat	Woodland and pasture, also scrub.
Food	Omnivorous; earthworms are an important part of its diet.
Range	Across most of Europe, except extreme north and some islands.
Similar species	None.

MONGOOSE *Herpestes ichneumon*

The Mongoose was introduced into Europe from North Africa. Its coarsely furred coat is uniformly greyish, the snout is pointed and the tail long and tapering. It is mainly active at night and rarely encountered, despite often living close to human habitation and raiding poultry. It nests in a rock cleft or burrow, and has 1 litter a year of up to 4 young.

Size	45–54 cm, plus a tail of up to 44 cm.
Habitat	Arid areas with thick scrub, also rocky hillsides.
Food	Omnivorous; mainly small animals, also eggs.
Range	S Spain and Portugal. Small Indian Mongoose, *H. auropunctatus*, was introduced into Croatia and adjacent islands, and Indian Grey Mongoose, *H. edwardsi*, was introduced into Italy.
Similar species	Western Polecat (p.100), and Beech Marten (p.102), which are shorter tailed.

RACCOON *Procyon lotor*

The Raccoon was introduced into Europe as a result of escapes from fur farms. The body fur is thick and grey, the tail bushy and striped, and the face has a distinctive 'robber's mask'. It is mainly active at night and does not hibernate. Despite its rather ungainly appearance it swims and climbs well. One litter of 1–7 young is born in spring.

Size	60–95 cm, plus a tail of up to 40 cm.
Habitat	Well-wooded country, often near water.
Food	Wide variety, including molluscs, fish, frogs, small mammals, birds and their eggs; also fruit and nuts.
Range	Still spreading; most common in Germany and around the Baltic states.
Similar species	Raccoon Dog (p.96) has longer legs and the tail is not banded.

WILD CAT *Felis sylvestris*

Larger than domestic cats, the Wild Cat has a proportionally bushier and blunter tail; it has 'tabby' markings. Mainly nocturnal, it is a good climber, but mostly hunts on the ground. It does not hibernate and usually has 1 litter, though it may have up to 3. The 1–8 young are born blind and helpless.

Size	46–78 cm, plus a tail of up to 38 cm.
Habitat	Forest and woodland; rocky and scrub habitats in the south of its range.
Food	Mammals up to the size of a lamb, birds and carrion.
Range	Patchily distributed through Europe, north to the Baltic states. Small numbers in Scotland, thought to be increasing.
Similar species	Domestic and feral cats.

LYNX *Lynx lynx*

This large cat has long legs, distinctive ear tufts and a stumpy, black-tipped tail. It is usually sandy coloured with variable spotting, the most heavily spotted animals occurring in the Carpathians, Eastern Europe. It is usually solitary and hunts mainly at night. The single litter is born in early summer and contains 1–4 young.

Size	70–150 cm, plus a tail of 12–24 cm.
Habitat	Forest, rocky slopes and scrub.
Food	Mammals up to the size of young deer and birds.
Range	Extinct over much of Europe, except Scandinavia and E Europe.
Similar species	Spanish Lynx (p.110), but ranges do not overlap. Wild Cat (opposite) and domestic cat are considerably smaller.

SPANISH LYNX *Lynx pardina*

The Spanish or Pardel Lynx is almost identical in appearance to the more heavily spotted form of the Lynx (p.109) that occurs in the Carpathians. The range of the Spanish Lynx is considerably reduced and it is now one of the most threatened of all European mammals.

Size	Similar to the Lynx, but generally slightly smaller.
Habitat	Open woodland and scrub.
Food	Mostly rabbits, but also deer, waterfowl, partridge, and small mammals and birds.
Range	Confined to S Spain and W Portugal; formerly more widespread.
Similar species	Lynx, but ranges do not overlap.

GENET *Genetta genetta*

This cat-like carnivore (shown investigating a Hedgehog) is about the same size as a domestic cat, but has a longer, banded tail and shorter legs; the fur is sandy-yellow and heavily spotted. It was introduced into Europe from North Africa. It is shy and elusive, making its lair in a hollow tree, rock cleft or among roots, and hunting at night. The single litter has 1–3 young.

Size 44–55 cm, plus a tail of up to 48 cm.
Habitat Woodland, scrub and open well-vegetated areas.
Food Birds and small mammals, also fruit and berries.
Range Widespread across Spain and Portugal, west into France; occurs on Mallorca.
Similar species Wild Cat and domestic cat.

WALRUS AND SEALS

Seals are highly specialised marine mammals sometimes classified with the carnivores. There are three groups: the sealions and fur seals (which do not occur in European waters), the Walrus, and the seals. Unlike the whales and dolphins (cetaceans), seals need to come to land in order to breed. In some cases the pup is able to swim within a few hours of birth, but most are confined to land for several weeks. Seals often haul out and bask in the sun on undisturbed shores. While on land seals are awkward and can only move with difficulty, but once in the water they are extremely agile. The Walrus, and several species of seal, breed on ice floes in the Arctic. They mostly have a single pup, often with a thick white fur that is moulted before it takes to the sea. The only seal to occur in the warmer waters of the Mediterranean is the Monk Seal, which is seriously endangered. It seems unlikely that it will survive because, in addition to persecution by fishermen, it is suffering from the effects of increased pollution, and being trapped in drifting fishing gear.

Harbour Seals often haul out on sand bars and shores, and bask in the sun

COMMON SEAL *Phoca vitulina*

This small seal has a concave muzzle and variable colouring, which is usually greyish with dense mottling; the whiskers are white. A single pup is born each year (in midsummer) on a beach or sand bar, and is suckled in the sea; they are active from birth.

Size	1.2–1.6 m.
Habitat	Inshore waters, including sea lochs and occasionally rivers.
Food	Mainly fish, also shellfish and crustaceans.
Range	Breeds around the British Isles, N France and north to Arctic Scandinavia and Iceland.
Similar species	Grey Seal (opposite) and Ringed Seal, *P. hispida*.

GREY SEAL *Halichoerus grypus*

The Grey Seal has a dog-like head and a convex profile. The male is larger and dark with light blotches; the female is paler with dark blotches. Large colonies congregate to breed and are very vocal, wailing and barking. The single pup is born on shore and has whitish, silky fur.

Size	1.65–2.3 m.
Habitat	Marine, but breeds on shore.
Food	Fish and crustaceans.
Range	Around coasts of the British Isles, N France, north to the Baltic, Scandinavia, the Russian states and Iceland.
Similar species	Common Seal (opposite) has a rounder head.

MEDITERRANEAN MONK SEAL Monachus monachus

The only seal which is chocolate brown (although males tend to be paler), the Monk Seal has a whitish patch on the belly. Now very rare, it is extremely shy and breeds on beaches of a few uninhabited islands. It is active by day and night. The single pup is born in summer or autumn, and has woolly, dark brown fur at birth.

Size	Up to 3 m.
Habitat	Marine and rocky beaches.
Food	Mainly fish, also octopus.
Range	Almost extinct in the W Mediterranean, only occurs in about 20 sites in the Mediterranean, Aegean and Black Seas.
Similar species	None.

HARP SEAL *Pagophilus groenlandicus*

The male Harp Seal is creamy-white with a blackish head and a characteristic darker marking, which is 'harp' shaped, across the back. The female's markings are less distinct. They congregate in large groups during the breeding season, when a single pup is born on the ice. It has thick yellowish fur and is active from birth.

Size	1.8–2 m.
Habitat	Marine; rarely south of 60° N in European waters.
Food	Mostly fish.
Range	Breeds in N Scandinavia and the Russian states. Occasionally wanders south as far as Britain and W Sweden.
Similar species	No other seals have the 'harp' marking.

117

HOODED SEAL *Cystophora cristata*

The Hooded Seal is large and greyish with variable paler markings; the female is generally lighter in colour. The male has a crest on the nose which it can inflate to form a large hood. A single pup is born each spring with white fur, which moults into bluish-grey soon after birth.

Size	1.8–2.5 m.
Habitat	Marine.
Food	Fish and squid.
Range	Breeds on Jan Mayan, near Spitzbergen and disperses south, occasionally as far as Britain.
Similar species	Often found with Harp Seals (p.117).

WALRUS *Odobenus rosmarus*

The Walrus is the largest seal in European waters. The male (also some females) is distinguished by its large (up to 1 m) tusks; it also has a 'moustache' of bristles on the snout. The greyish skin is thick and wrinkled. They congregate in large herds on the ice to breed, and pups can swim within a few hours of birth.

Size	Up to 2.5 m.
Habitat	Marine, close to Arctic ice.
Food	Bivalve molluscs, and occasionally seals.
Range	Patchy distribution in North Atlantic and Arctic Oceans; occasionally south to Iceland, Norway and, more rarely, Britain.
Similar species	None.

HOOFED MAMMALS

There are two groups of ungulates, or hoofed mammals: the odd-toed (horses, rhinos and tapirs), and the even-toed (cattle, sheep, deer and their relatives). Only the latter occur in a truly wild state in Europe. Ungulates are generally large, and they are all herbivorous, either grazing or browsing vegetation. Most of them have horns, which are used by the males for fighting in the breeding season (rut). They are mostly gregarious, living in herds or flocks, and the young are active from birth, often joining the herd within a few hours of birth. Nearly all the species are hunted, and in some cases they owe their survival to this fact. The earliest wildlife protection laws were usually concerned with protecting deer, bison and other ungulates, in order that they could be hunted. In areas where they are protected they are often relatively easily seen, but elsewhere they are often shy and active by night.

Many hoofed animals, such as Red Deer, form herds, particularly during the rut

WILD BOAR *Sus scrofa*

The Wild Boar is the ancestor of the domestic pig and although extinct or rare over much of Europe, it has been successfully protected and reintroduced as a game animal in many areas. The adult is covered with coarse dark brown hair, and has prominent tusks; the young have pale longitudinal stripes.

Size	1.1–1.8 m, plus a tail of up to 25 cm.
Habitat	Forest, woodland and farmland.
Food	Omnivorous.
Range	Widespread over most of Europe, north to S Scandinavia. Extinct in British Isles.
Similar species	Domestic pigs, when allowed to roam free in woodland.

BISON *Bison bonasus*

The largest European land animal, the Bison has humped shoulders, curving horns and shaggy, dark brown fur. Once widespread, it became extinct in the wild in the early 20th century, but has been reintroduced. It lives in herds, which are mainly active by day, but it often feeds at dusk and dawn. A single calf is born every other year, and is lighter in colour.

Size	2.5–3.5 m, plus a tail of up to 80 cm.
Habitat	Forest and woodland.
Food	Leaves, twigs and other vegetation.
Range	The Bialowieza Forest in Poland and a few other reserves in the Russian states, Poland and Romania.
Similar species	None.

123

MUSK OX *Ovibos moschatus*

The Musk Ox (a relative of the sheep) is native to North America and Greenland, but has been introduced into Europe. Its fur is dark brown, long and shaggy, and the horns are downward curving. They congregate in herds of up to 100. The female gives birth to a single young in the summer.

Size	2–2.5 m, plus a tail of up to 19 cm.
Habitat	Arctic tundra.
Food	Sedges, grasses and shrubs.
Range	Two areas of N-central Norway (Dovrefjell) and Sweden (Harjedalen).
Similar species	None.

MOUFLON *Ovis musimon*

Although an ancestor of the domestic sheep, the Mouflon lacks the woolly fleece. It is dark above, paler below and the male usually has a paler patch on the flanks (saddle) and heavy, curled horns. It is mainly active by day, but often at night in hot weather; in winter it may descend to lower altitudes.

Size	80 cm–1.25 m, plus a tail of up to 15 cm.
Habitat	Deciduous and mixed woodland, and mountain grassland.
Food	Herbs and grasses.
Range	Corsica and Sardinia; successfully reintroduced into many other parts of mainland Europe, and now widespread.
Similar species	Domestic sheep.

ALPINE IBEX *Capra ibex*

This member of the goat family is darkish-brown above with a paler belly and both sexes carry horns, although they are much longer in the male. During the rut males charge each other, clashing horns; females and young form their own groups. It is mainly active by day, and moves to lower altitudes in winter.

Size	1.15–1.7 m, plus a tail of up to 20 cm.
Habitat	Mountains, usually above the tree line.
Food	Mainly grasses, also twigs, bark and berries.
Range	Nearly exterminated during the 19th century, a population survives in Gran Paradiso National Park (Italy). Successful reintroduction in the Alps.
Similar species	Chamois (p.129) and domestic goat. Spanish Ibex, *C. pyrenaica*, but its range does not overlap.

WILD GOAT *Capra aegagrus*

The most pure-bred ancestor of the domestic goat is found only on two Greek islands – other European wild goats have interbred with domestic goats for centuries. The Wild Goat is brown above, paler below and has a blackish stripe along the shoulders and back. A single young is born in spring.

Size	1.2–1.6 m, plus a tail of up to 20 cm.
Habitat	Rocky hillsides.
Food	A wide range of vegetation.
Range	Crete and other Greek islands.
Similar species	Feral Goat (p.128) in many parts of Europe.

FERAL GOAT *Capra hircus*

Feral Goats vary enormously in appearance. Those in the British Isles are generally long haired, and often black and white. Their horns twist outwards (not backwards, as in the wild goats). In behaviour and breeding they are very similar to the wild species, and are often very shy and elusive.

Size	About 1.5 m, plus a tail of up to 20 cm.
Habitat	Rocky hillsides in the Mediterranean; upland and moorland in British Isles.
Food	A wide range of vegetation.
Range	Main populations in Ireland, Scotland, Wales and around the Mediterranean, particularly on Greek islands.
Similar species	Wild Goat (p.127) and Alpine Ibex (p.126).

CHAMOIS *Rupicapra rupicapra*

The fur of the Chamois is light brown in summer, turning almost black in winter; the face is black and white. Both sexes carry slender horns, which are short and curve sharply backwards at the ends. They are gregarious and form large herds in the winter. A single lamb, occasionally twins or triplets, is born in the summer.

Size	90–140 cm, plus a tail of up to 8 cm.
Habitat	Pastures near tree line in summer; valleys in winter.
Food	Grasses and herbs; also browses on trees.
Range	Isolated populations from N Spain through France, Italy and C Europe to the Carpathians, and south to the Balkans.
Similar species	Alpine Ibex (p.126), domestic sheep and goats.

129

RED DEER *Cervus elaphus*

Variable in size and colouring, the Red Deer is usually reddish-brown in summer and more greyish in winter; fawns are heavily spotted. The male has large, branching antlers and develops a shaggy mane during the rut, when its loud roars can be heard. It is mainly active by night (sometimes by day), and often lives close to humans.

Size	1.7–2.6 m, plus a tail of up to 15 cm.
Habitat	Forest, woodland; also more open habitats.
Food	Grasses, shoots, twigs, leaves and bark.
Range	Widespread over much of Europe, from Spain and Portugal to Scandinavia.
Similar species	Other deer, particularly Sika (opposite) and Fallow (p.132).

SIKA DEER *Cervus nippon*

The Sika Deer is similar to the Red Deer (opposite), but smaller, and has a spotted coat in summer whereas the Red Deer is only spotted as a fawn. The two species occasionally interbreed. The single fawn (occasionally twins), born in early summer, is heavily spotted, and active soon after birth.

Size	1–1.55 m, plus a tail of up to 27 cm.
Habitat	Woodland, forest and parkland.
Food	Leaves and shoots.
Range	Introduced from Asia into many parts of Europe, including the British Isles and Ireland. Range is spreading.
Similar species	Red Deer.

131

FALLOW DEER *Dama dama*

The Fallow Deer varies widely from buff-brown with whitish spots on the back to a more uniform white to blackish colour. The male's antlers are thick and flattened (palmate), and the tail is longish with a black line down the centre. They live in herds and produce 1 (occasionally 2) heavily spotted fawns a year.

Size	1.3–2.4 m, plus a tail of up to 20 cm.
Habitat	Parkland and open woodland.
Food	Grasses, leaves and shoots.
Range	Partly domesticated, occurs widely across Europe, both in the wild and parkland.
Similar species	Red Deer (p.130).

WHITE-TAILED DEER *Odocoileus virginianus*

This deer is reddish-brown in summer and greyish-brown in winter. The tail is thick and bushy, and white below; when alarmed it flicks it, exposing the white on the tail and white rump. The male's antlers are wide and curve inwards at the tips. A single fawn is born in the summer, with maybe a litter of 2–3 in the second year.

Size	1.3–2 m, plus a tail of up to 33 cm.
Habitat	Woodland.
Food	Grasses, twigs, leaves and shoots.
Range	An American species, introduced into Finland – appears to be spreading. Also introduced into the Czech Republic and former Yugoslavia.
Similar species	Red Deer (p.130).

133

SPOTTED DEER *Cervus axis*

Both male and female Spotted Deer (also known as Chital and Axis Deer) have spotted coats throughout the year. The male carries wide antlers (growing up to 1 m), which are sparsely branched, and during the rut males will fight fiercely. They are prolific breeders and the female may have more than one fawn a year.

Size Up to 1.7 m.

Habitat Open woodland near water.

Food Browses on leaves of shrubs; also grazes on grass and herbage.

Range Introduced into the former Yugoslavia from Asia.

Similar species Fallow Deer (p.132).

ELK *Alces alces*

This large deer, known as the Moose in North America, has a dark brown body with pale legs. The male carries broad, flattened (palmate) antlers and will fight for females during the rut. They are solitary or live in small family groups and are agile on land and in water. The young (usually 2, but can be up to 4) are born in early summer.

Size	2–3.1 m, plus a tail of about 5 cm.
Habitat	Wet woodland and swamps.
Food	Browses on trees; also aquatic vegetation.
Range	Widespread in Scandinavia, around the Baltic to Poland, spreading southwards.
Similar species	None.

REINDEER *Rangifer tarandus*

The Reindeer is greyish to greyish-white, and both males and females carry antlers, which have a forward sweeping branch and, unlike any other deer, have a second branch near the top. They are active by day and night and often form large herds. The single calf is born in spring and is active soon after birth. Reindeer have been domesticated on a large scale.

Size	1.7–2.2 m, plus a tail of up to 18 cm.
Habitat	Arctic tundra and woodland.
Food	Lichens, shoots, grasses, sedges and leaves.
Range	Reduced to small populations in Scandinavia and eastwards through Russia. Domestic herds elsewhere not uncommon (eg Scotland).
Similar species	Domestic reindeer usually smaller and colour varies more.

ROE DEER *Capreolus capreolus*

The smallest native European deer, the Roe Deer is rich reddish-brown, turning greyer in winter. The male carries short, spiky antlers; both sexes have a barking call. Although usually active by night, when not disturbed they are also active by day. The single litter has up to 3 fawns (usually 2), which are heavily spotted.

Size	90–130 cm, plus a tail of up to 3.5 cm.
Habitat	Woodland and forest.
Food	Grasses, shoots and leaves.
Range	Widespread across Europe, including parts of Great Britain, but absent from most islands.
Similar species	Chinese Water Deer (p.139) and Muntjac (p.138).

REEVES' MUNTJAC *Muntiacus reevesi*

This small, stocky deer was introduced into England from Asia, as a result of escapes from wildlife parks. Uniformly mid- to dark brown, the broad tail conceals a white rump, which is only visible when it runs away. The male has short antlers and small tusks. It is also known as the Barking Deer, as it emits a dog-like bark loudly and repeatedly.

Size	70–90 cm, plus a tail of up to 12 cm.
Habitat	Woodland and gardens, often suburban.
Food	Wide variety of vegetation, including shoots, grasses and leaves; also garden plants and fruit.
Range	Widespread and locally abundant in S and E England.
Similar species	Chinese Water Deer (opposite) and Roe Deer (p.137).

CHINESE WATER DEER *Hydropotes inermis*

Generally a uniform sandy-brown, this is the only deer in Europe that lack antlers in both sexes; the male, however, has quite prominent tusks. It is mainly active by night. The male has a whistling call during the rut, and it 'screams' when alarmed. The single litter is born in late spring, with up to 6 (usually 2–4) spotted fawns.

Size	75–105 cm, plus a tail of up to 8 cm.
Habitat	Marshes, woodland and parkland.
Food	Shoots, leaves and grass.
Range	Introduced into S and E England (where it is spreading) and one locality in France, as a result of escapes from wildlife parks.
Similar species	Muntjac (opposite) and Roe Deer (p.137).

WHALES AND DOLPHINS

There are two groups of cetaceans: the toothed whales (including the dolphins and porpoises) and the baleen whales. The latter lack teeth and feed by filtering fish and plankton through horny plates of baleen. The baleen whales are all large, and include the largest mammal known, the Blue Whale, which grows to a length of 33 m, and a weight of 190,000 kg. The largest of the toothed whales is the Sperm Whale. Cetaceans are all entirely aquatic, even giving birth at sea; the young have to surface within minutes of birth in order to breathe, and are able to follow the mother. Some dolphins are gregarious, and may live in schools numbering several hundred. The toothed whales use sonar (similar to bats) to navigate and hunt their prey. Some of the baleen whales use 'songs' to communicate over many miles. However, the evidence of whales using their sonar or songs for true communication is doubtful. Nearly every species of cetacean is threatened or endangered. The larger species (and some of the smaller) have been hunted to the brink of extinction, and thousands are killed in nets set for tuna and other fish, trapped in broken nets drifting the oceans, and some are probably poisoned by eating polluted fish. Generally rather difficult to observe, some whales can be very active on the surface of the sea: Humpback Whales are often seen jumping clear of the water (right), and even somersaulting. In the middle of their back cetaceans often have a boneless fin, called the dorsal fin.

FIN WHALE *Balaenoptera physalus*

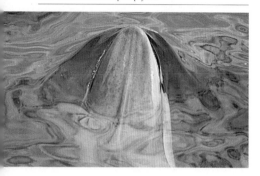

The Fin Whale (or Common Rorqual) is unusual in having asymmetrical colouring – the right side of the lower jaw is pale, the left is dark. It is large and slender with a small dorsal fin. It travels singly or in pods (groups) of up to 15, and moves to tropical waters in the winter. A single young is born every other year.

Size	Up to 26.8 m.
Habitat	Marine.
Food	Small fish and plankton.
Range	Formerly widespread in European waters. Now seen most often off the Hebrides, Iceland and east to Norway, less often in the Mediterranean.
Similar species	Blue Whale (opposite), which is not asymmetrically marked.

BLUE WHALE *Baleanoptera musculus*

This is the largest mammal in the world, and like other rorquals it is streamlined and has grooves on its throat. The dorsal fin is extremely small and when it surfaces after diving it emerges almost horizontally. When breathing out it emits a single cone of mist up to 12 m high. A single calf is born every 3 years.

Size	Up to 33 m, but rarely above 27 m.
Habitat	Marine.
Food	Krill and plankton.
Range	Once widespread, now extremely rare. Most likely seen in Atlantic waters.
Similar species	Fin Whale (p.142).

HUMPBACK WHALE *Megaptera novaeangliae*

A distinctive whale which frequently throws itself out of the water (breaching), becoming clearly visible. It has huge flippers (up to 5 m long) with scalloped edges, and the dorsal fin, set back towards the end of the body, is followed by a series of bumps. It is very playful in the water, often turning backward somersaults. It normally travels in pods of 3 or 4.

Size	Up to 19 m.
Habitat	Marine.
Food	Small fish.
Range	Extremely rare in most European waters; may be increasing in W Atlantic.
Similar species	None.

SPERM WHALE *Physeter catodon*

The Sperm Whale is the largest toothed whale, having peg-like teeth on the lower jaw only. It has a large, square-shaped head, and broad, triangular tail flukes. Its social structure is such that when one is injured, or a female is giving birth, others will come to help. A single calf (occasionally twins) is born every 4 years, in winter.

Size	Up to 20 m, usually 11–15 m.
Habitat	Marine.
Food	Squid and octopus, also some fish.
Range	Only in European waters (particularly the Mediterranean) in summer, when they occur north to the Arctic.
Similar species	None.

145

WHITE WHALE *Delphinapterus leucas*

Also known as the Beluga, it is pure white, although the calf is grey, turning white as it matures. The head is rounded, and there is no dorsal fin. Some populations migrate north in the summer. A single calf is born every 2–3 years. White Whales have been known to live for 50 years.

Size	Up to 4.6 m.
Habitat	Marine.
Food	Fish and crustaceans.
Range	Confined to colder Arctic waters; occasionally strays into European waters.
Similar species	No other whale is pure white.

LONG-FINNED PILOT WHALE *Globicephala melaena*

This whale has a rounded head and a large, curved dorsal fin. The body is black or dark grey with a paler patch under the fin, and the underside is white. It moves south in the winter, often in pods of up to 200, and makes a variety of noises, including clicks, squeaks and whistles.

Size	Up to 8.5 m.
Habitat	Marine.
Food	Squid and fish.
Range	Widespread, but declining in the North Atlantic, North Sea and Mediterranean.
Similar species	Short-Finned Pilot Whale, *G. macrorhynchus*, from tropical waters has been recorded in European waters.

KILLER WHALE *Orcinus orca*

The Killer Whale, or Orca, has a large, triangular dorsal fin (up to 2 m high), which can be seen cutting through the water as it swims close to the surface. It has distinctive black and white markings, and is carnivorous with long, conical teeth. It travels in pods of up to 20 and will prey on other whales.

Size	Up to 9.75 m.
Habitat	Marine.
Food	Sea mammals, including whales and seals; also birds, fish and squid.
Range	Widespread in Atlantic Ocean, North and Baltic Seas and Mediterranean.
Similar species	None.

BOTTLE-NOSED DOLPHIN *Tursiops truncatus*

These dolphins are bluish-grey above and paler below, with spotted flanks. The dorsal fin is tall and slender, and the beak is short, but prominent. Although relatively slow swimmers, they are playful and gregarious. They are mainly marine, but can occur in lagoons, bays and rivers. This is the species most often exhibited in aquariums.

Size	Up to 4 m.
Habitat	Marine.
Food	Fish and crustaceans.
Range	Common and widespread in Atlantic and Mediterranean. Also occurs in other European seas.
Similar species	Rough-toothed Dolphin, *Steno bredanesis*, is much rarer. Striped Dolphin, *Stenella coeruleoalba*, has more distinctive beak and lacks spots.

149

COMMON DOLPHIN *Delphinus delphis*

The Common Dolphin is tri-coloured: dark grey above, white below, with bands of paler grey and yellowish-fawn on the sides; the eye patch is usually black. Schools of up to 250,000 were once recorded, but numbers have declined considerably. A single calf is born every 2–3 years, and they can live to over 30 years.

Size	Up to 2.6 m.
Habitat	Marine.
Food	Squid and fish.
Range	Widespread in all European seas.
Similar species	Other dolphins are less common and lack the yellowish colouring on the sides.

HARBOUR PORPOISE *Phocoena phocoena*

This small, compact whale has a blunt head, no beak and a small dorsal fin. It is grey above, whitish below and has a characteristic rolling movement, rarely leaping clear of the water. A single calf is born every other year. Hunting, drowning in fishing tackle and pesticide poisoning have led to a dramatic decline of numbers.

Size	Up to 1.8 m.
Habitat	Coastal marine estuaries.
Food	Fish, also crustaceans and squid.
Range	Widespread, but depleted numbers, from the Atlantic to the Arctic Ocean. Also in Baltic Sea.
Similar species	None.

SALAMANDERS AND NEWTS

The tailed amphibians are all long-bodied, and usually have moist skins. The term 'salamander' is used to indicate the largely terrestrial species, while 'newt' is confined to those that spend much of the year in water. Unlike salamanders, male newts have crests during the breeding season, which range from simple ridges to long, flowing crests, and are used in elaborate courtship displays. Most species are active at night, and are more easily observed with a torch, on warm summer evenings after heavy rain, when both newts and salamanders may be seen foraging on land. Newts can be easily observed by torchlight in ponds.

Most newts and salamanders lay eggs, though some retain the eggs within the body until they are ready to hatch, or even produce fully metamorphosed young. (The change from the larval 'tadpole' to the adult is known as metamorphosis.) The tadpoles are distinguished from those of frogs and toads by their feathery external gills, and the forelegs develop much earlier. Some populations and species are neotenous – that is, they retain the characters of the juveniles throughout their life.

Like most tailed amphibians, the larva (tadpole) of the Great Crested Newt has large, feathery gills

FIRE SALAMANDER *Salamandra salamandra*

The Fire Salamander is black with varying amounts of yellow, orange or reddish markings; it is sometimes striped. Mainly active at night, it is normally only seen after rain. The tadpoles are born well developed, sometimes fully metamorphosed.

Size	Up to 20 cm, including tail.
Habitat	Usually damp, forested areas close to water.
Food	Slow-moving invertebrates such as worms and molluscs; also small amphibians.
Range	Widespread over most of Europe, except north and east; absent from British Isles.
Similar species	Alpine Salamander (opposite) lacks yellow markings.

ALPINE SALAMANDER *Salamandra atra*

A uniformly black salamander, usually active and visible after rain at night; at other times it hides under logs and rocks. Because of the short summers in its habitat, the young (usually 2–4) are born fully metamorphosed, but may take up to 4 years to develop inside the mother.

Size	Up to 16 cm, including tail.
Habitat	Usually in wooded, mountainous habitats, mostly between 800–2,000 m, but up to 3,000 m.
Food	Invertebrates.
Range	The Alps, east to the former Yugoslavia and Albania.
Similar species	Fire Salamander (opposite) usually has spotting.

GOLDEN-STRIPED SALAMANDER *Chioglossa lusitanica*

A remarkably agile salamander, it runs swiftly when disturbed, hiding among rocks, or diving into water where it is a strong swimmer. It can shed its long tail, in a manner similar to lizards, and the tail is usually smoother and greyer when it regrows. It uses its long, sticky tongue to catch its prey.

Size	Up to 15 cm, including a long tail.
Habitat	Mountainous regions, mainly in wooded areas close to streams.
Food	Invertebrates.
Range	Only in a relatively small area of Spain and Portugal.
Similar species	Most likely to be confused with lizards.

SHARP-RIBBED SALAMANDER *Pleurodeles waltl*

A large, rather heavily built, salamander. It has a row of orange warts along its side, and the ribs sometimes protrude through them. It is mostly active by night and aquatic, burrowing under stones in summer when the ponds and streams dry up. The male has pads on its forelegs during the breeding season.

Size	Up to 30 cm, including tail.
Habitat	Normally in or close to water.
Food	Invertebrates, and other small aquatic animals, including tadpoles.
Range	Only in Spain and Portugal.
Similar species	None in its range.

PYRENEAN BROOK SALAMANDER *Euproctus asper*

A medium-sized salamander with a flattened appearance. The skin is rather granular and rough, and the eyes are relatively small. Although mainly active by night, it sometimes emerges during the day, but is rarely found away from water and often hides under stones, and even in caves.

Size	Up to 16 cm, including tail.
Habitat	Cold mountain streams at altitudes of up to 2,500 m.
Food	Invertebrates.
Range	Confined to the Pyrenees. Tend to be rare in streams with trout, which eat them.
Similar species	Only likely to be confused with Sharp-ribbed Salamander (p.157), which is absent from the Pyrenees. However, two closely related species occur on the islands of Corsica and Sardinia. The Corsican Brook Salamander, *E. montanus*, and the Sardinian Brook Salamander, *E. platycephalus*, are similar to the Pyrenean Brook Salamander, but males sometimes have blunt 'spurs' on the hind limbs, which are used when mating, and they often have a reddish-brown stripe down the centre of the back.

Marbled Newt *Triturus marmoratus*

A beautifully coloured newt, with bright green markings on the back, which appears velvety outside the breeding season. The underside is greyish, and females and young have an orange stripe down the back. Like other newts it is totally aquatic in the breeding season, and the breeding males have a striped crest.

Size Up to 16 cm, including tail.

Habitat Always within reach of water for breeding, but often in relatively dry areas, including woodland and heaths.

Food Invertebrates.

Range Confined to Portugal, Spain and W France, where it is fairly common.

Similar species None.

CRESTED NEWT *Triturus cristatus*

A large newt, generally found in or close to water. It has a rather warty skin, which is usually black above and bright yellow or orange, with black markings, below. When breeding the male is paler above, with a large, jagged crest. In the south of its range it is usually found at higher altitudes.

Size	Up to 18 cm, but usually less.
Habitat	Wide variety, usually close to water. Generally breeds in deep ponds, or slow-flowing streams.
Food	Invertebrates, eggs and young of amphibians, and probably fish fry.
Range	Widespread over most of N Europe; in Britain it has declined in many areas.
Similar species	Other closely related crested newts over most of the rest of Europe.

161

ALPINE NEWT *Triturus alpestris*

A medium-sized newt with a much wider distribution than its name suggests. It is dark above, often blackish when on land, with a bright, unspotted, orange belly. Some populations are neotenous (see p.152), retaining gills throughout their life. It is only found in mountains in the south of its range, but at sea level in the north.

Size	Up to 12 cm.
Habitat	Always close to water, and often aquatic all year.
Food	Invertebrates, and probably fish and amphibian eggs and fry.
Range	Widespread in C Europe. Isolated populations in Spain and former Yugoslavia. Introduced in Britain.
Similar species	Crested Newt (p.161) usually has black on belly.

SMOOTH NEWT *Triturus vulgaris*

Generally the most widespread and abundant newt over most of its range. It is relatively small and the orange belly is usually spotted. In the breeding season the male develops a very large, wavy crest along the body and tail. Like most other newts, it leaves the water after breeding, and the skin becomes dryish and velvety, and it may be confused with a lizard. They normally hide under logs and stones.

Size	Up to 11 cm, but often much smaller.
Habitat	Almost any habitat close to breeding waters.
Food	Invertebrates, probably fish fry and amphibian eggs.
Range	Widespread over most of Europe, except the SW.
Similar species	Other small newts are usually not as heavily spotted below.

163

PALMATE NEWT *Triturus helveticus*

A small newt, easily confused with the Smooth Newt (p.163) as their ranges mostly overlap. The Palmate Newt is generally slightly smaller, less spotted on the belly, and the breeding male has only a slight crest, confined to the tail. However, the male has distinctive blackish hind feet, and its tail ends in a filament.

Size	Up to 9 cm, but often smaller.
Habitat	Favours rather acid, clear water for breeding; sometimes even brackish water.
Food	Invertebrates.
Range	Confined to NW Europe.
Similar species	Other small newts.

SARDINIAN CAVE SALAMANDER *Speleomantes genei*

The Sardinian Cave Salamander is medium-sized, with characteristic partially webbed feet that make the toes appear short and stubby. The colouring is rather variable, but it is generally brownish with lighter spotting. It is agile and climbs well. Its prey is caught by an extendable sticky tongue.

Size	Up to 13 cm, including tail.
Habitat	Confined to humid, cool caves.
Food	Invertebrates.
Range	Occurs only on Sardinia.
Similar species	Some classifications divide the Sardinian Cave Salamander into several species.

ITALIAN CAVE SALAMANDER *Speleomantes italicus*

Similar in general appearance to the Sardinian Cave Salamander, this salamander usually has brighter, more clearly defined markings, often with white marbling on the underside. The cave salamanders' closest relatives are found in California, and they are all characterised by not having lungs – they breathe through the skin and mouth.

Size	Up to 12 cm, including tail; often smaller.
Habitat	Restricted to damp rocky places, including caves.
Food	Invertebrates.
Range	Restricted to N Italy.
Similar species	A closely-related species, *S. ambrosii*, occurs in N Italy & SE France.

OLM *Proteus anguinus*

This large, unmistakable aquatic salamander, is white or pinkish-white with feathery gills. The eyes are vestigial, and the legs and feet are also much reduced. It is neotenous (see p.152), spending its entire life in cold water. It lays up to 70 eggs, but may retain them in the body until the young (usually 2) are produced.

Size	Up to 25 cm, including tail.
Habitat	Underground lakes and streams.
Food	Invertebrates.
Range	Only in the karst caves in the former Yugoslavia and adjacent Italy, where it is threatened by pollution and disturbance.
Similar species	None.

FROGS AND TOADS

The name 'frog' is generally applied to the smooth-skinned species of amphibians, while the 'toad' has rough, warty skin. They are all short-bodied, lack tails and have significantly longer back legs than forelegs. Most of them jump, and some species are able to jump a metre or more. Some species have a paratoid gland, a large swollen area behind the eye, containing poisons. Some salamanders also have these glands. All frogs and toads except the midwife toad migrate to water during the breeding season, where they lay spawn in clumps, or long strings, which hatches into tadpoles. In a few species the tadpoles grow very large – larger even than the adults. The group of frogs known collectively as 'green frogs' are very aquatic, and their classification is extremely complex since it involves hybrid populations. These, and several other species, can be particularly difficult to identify, but during the breeding season the males have distinctive mating calls. These sounds are often amplified by inflatable vocal sacs – either a single one under the chin, or a pair either side of the head.

Frogs and toads, including the Common Frog, often return year after year to the same communal breeding ponds

YELLOW-BELLIED TOAD *Bombina variegata*

A small, distinctive toad, which is often very abundant. It is distinguished from other species by its contrasting yellow and black underside. During the breeding season the male's voice is a musical *poop-poop-poop*, given in chorus with other males. It is active by day and night, and can often be seen swimming in its breeding pool.

Size	Up to 5 cm.
Habitat	Usually around ponds and ditches, in well-vegetated areas, including woodland.
Food	Mostly invertebrates.
Range	Widespread from W France to E Europe and Italy.
Similar species	Fire-bellied Toad (opposite) is only other toad with bright coloured underside.

FIRE-BELLIED TOAD *Bombina bombina*

Similar in appearance to the Yellow-bellied Toad (opposite), but this toad has black and red markings on the underside. The male's call is also similar, but slower and more mournful. Where the two species' ranges overlap, the Fire-bellied Toad tends to occur in the more lowland areas. When attacked it may flip itself upside down to expose its belly, as a warning to predators that its skin contains poisons.

Size	Up to 5 cm.
Habitat	Similar to Yellow-bellied Toad, but at lower altitudes.
Food	Usually invertebrates.
Range	From E Europe as far west as Germany and Slovenia.
Similar species	Yellow-bellied Toad.

PAINTED FROG *Discoglossus pictus*

A small, attractively marked frog, related to the midwife and fire-bellied toads. These species all have round tongues that cannot be protruded like those of most other frogs and toads. Although rather similar to true frogs (*Rana* species), the Painted Frog has a triangular or round pupil, never a horizontal slit. During the breeding season, the male's call is a quiet *rar-rar-rar*.

Size	Up to about 7 cm.
Habitat	Usually close to water, including marshes and brackish water; breeds in ponds or slow-flowing streams.
Food	Invertebrates.
Range	Sicily and Malta, and also a small area of S France.
Similar species	Other painted frogs, but ranges do not overlap.

MIDWIFE TOAD *Alyetes obstetricans*

This small toad has prominent eyes with a vertical pupil (most frogs and toads have a horizontal pupil). It is named for its breeding behaviour: the male carries the spawn wrapped around its hind legs, taking it to water to keep it moist and depositing it in shallow water when the tadpoles are ready to hatch. The call is a bell-like *poo-poo-poo*, very similar to that of the Scops Owl.

Size	Up to 5 cm.
Habitat	Woodland, gardens and hedgerows; hides in burrows during the day.
Food	Invertebrates.
Range	W Europe; introduced into England.
Similar species	Yellow- and fire-bellied toads (pp.170 & 171), but these are brightly coloured on the underside.

IBERIAN MIDWIFE TOAD *Alyetes cisternasii*

This is a relatively little-known species. It is heavier built than the more widespread Midwife Toad (p.173). The easiest way to distinguish them is by the palms of the hands: the Iberian has two tubercles on the palm, the other species three. In common with the Midwife Toad, it is usually active by night, spending the day in a burrow, and its breeding behaviour is also similar.

Size	Up to 5 cm.
Habitat	Wide variety of rather sandy habitats.
Food	Invertebrates.
Range	Confined to S Portugal and C Spain.
Similar species	Midwife Toad.

COMMON SPADEFOOT *Pelobates fuscus*

This toad is distinguished from the true toads by having a vertical pupil. The hind feet have 'spurs', which are used for digging burrows up to 1 m deep. It likes sandy soils suitable for digging, and when captured it exudes a strong smell of garlic. Breeding males make a repeated clicking sound. When fully grown, the tadpoles are over twice the length of the adults – up to 18 cm.

Size	Up to 8 cm.
Habitat	Cultivated areas, coastal dunes.
Food	Invertebrates.
Range	Widespread from France and C Europe eastwards to Siberia, but declining in many areas.
Similar species	Other spadefoots.

175

PARSLEY FROG *Pelodytes punctatus*

A small, rather slender species, with warts forming lines on the back. Its colour varies, but is usually greyish-brown with parsley-green spots. It is an agile jumper and swimmer, and can climb smooth surfaces by using its damp belly as a sucker. The hind feet have long toes, with only slight webbing between them. Like the spadefoots, it is active by night, and often smells of garlic when handled.

Size	Up to 5 cm.
Habitat	Usually damp areas along streams and hedges.
Food	Invertebrates.
Range	Confined to France (and adjacent countries), Spain and Portugal.
Similar species	Most likely to be confused with other small frogs, which do not have warty skins.

COMMON TOAD *Bufo bufo*

A relatively large, robust species with an extremely warty skin and large paratoid glands (see p.168). As with all true toads and frogs, the pupil is a horizontal slit in bright light. Its colour changes slightly to match its surroundings. During the breeding season males gather in shallow water, and have a rather soft call. The eggs are laid in long strings, usually wrapped around waterweed.

Size	Up to 15 cm; larger in south of range.
Habitat	Almost all habitats, except extreme cold mountain tops and Arctic.
Food	Invertebrates, and other small animals.
Range	Across Europe, except Ireland and N Scandinavia.
Similar species	Most other toads are more brightly coloured.

177

NATTERJACK *Bufo calamita*

A small, relatively short-limbed toad, that tends to run rather than hop. It is easily recognised by the thin yellow stripe down the middle of the back. Breeding males gather around breeding pools and their calls can be heard for 2 km or more. Each call is a rapid ratchet-like sound, but several hundred merge into a continuous sound.

Size	Up to 10 cm, but usually smaller in north of range.
Habitat	Usually rather sandy areas, including sand dunes.
Food	Invertebrates.
Range	From Portugal and Spain east to the Baltic and S Sweden; also England and S Ireland, where it was probably introduced.
Similar species	Other toads usually lack yellow stripe.

GREEN TOAD *Bufo viridis*

A heavily built toad with prominent paratoid glands (see p. 168), and generally very attractively marked with green patches on a pale background. When breeding, the male has a high-pitched trilling call. Outside the breeding season, the Green Toad can often be seen hunting around lamp standards and other artificial lights, which attract large numbers of moths and other flying insects.

Size	Up to 10 cm.
Habitat	Usually relatively dry, lowland areas.
Food	Invertebrates.
Range	Widespread over E Europe, and as far west as NE France.
Similar species	Other toads usually lack the attractive markings.

179

COMMON TREE FROG *Hyla arborea*

A very small, brightly coloured frog, with pads on the ends of the fingers and toes. The back is usually brilliant green, but can be a blotchy brown or yellow. It is distinguished from other tree frogs by a dark, often cream-edged, stripe along the sides, from the eardrum to the hind leg. It often basks in full sun, relying on its colouring for camouflage.

Size	Up to 5 cm, but usually smaller.
Habitat	Usually close to water, in reeds or bushes, where it climbs extensively.
Food	Invertebrates.
Range	Widespread over most of Europe, except the north, British Isles and parts of Spain and Portugal.
Similar species	Stripeless Tree Frog (opposite). Tree frogs of Corsica and Sardinia may be a separate species, *H. sarda*.

STRIPELESS TREE FROG *Hyla meridionalis*

This frog is very similar in habits and colouring to the Common Tree Frog (opposite), but, as the name implies, it lacks the stripe along the flanks. The call of the male is similar, a repeated *krak, krak, krak*, but is slower, deeper, more resonant, and repeated less frequently. Where their ranges overlap, the Stripeless Tree Frog tends to occur at lower altitudes.

Size	Up to 5 cm.
Habitat	Usually well-vegetated areas close to water.
Food	Invertebrates.
Range	Confined to S France, Spain and Portugal, and extreme NW Italy.
Similar species	Other tree frogs.

COMMON FROG *Rana temporaria*

The Common Frog is one of the most widespread and often the most abundant amphibian in Europe; it is extremely tolerant of the cold. Its colour varies, being yellowish, brown or reddish. Compared with other frogs, it has relatively short hind limbs, but is still a powerful jumper. When breeding, the male has black thumb pads for clasping the female. The call is rather quiet and is produced under water.

Size	Up to 10 cm, but usually smaller.
Habitat	Almost all places with suitable breeding waters.
Food	Invertebrates.
Range	Across Europe, including the Arctic Circle, except most of Spain and Portugal.
Similar species	Other frogs.

MOOR FROG *Rana arvalis*

Very similar to the Common Frog (opposite), the Moor Frog has proportionately shorter hind limbs. The snout is more pointed and it generally has a rather striped pattern. It is found in moorland habitats such as meadows, bogs and fens, but rarely occurs at high altitudes.

Size	Up to 8 cm.
Habitat	Meadows, moors and similar damp places.
Food	Invertebrates.
Range	N and E Europe.
Similar species	Other frogs.

AGILE FROG *Rana dalmatina*

A relatively slender, long-legged frog, the Agile Frog is usually a delicate brownish above and pale below. It is a powerful jumper, often taking to the water when alarmed or pursued. It is usually found close to water, in fairly damp habitats, where its colouring makes it look like dead leaves.

Size	Up to 9 cm.
Habitat	Wet meadows, woodland.
Food	Invertebrates.
Range	From France, east to Romania, and south to Italy and Greece.
Similar species	Other frogs have shorter hind limbs.

IBERIAN MARSH FROG *Rana perezi*

A large frog, usually with extensive amounts of green on its back. It is often seen basking in the sun, either floating at the water's edge, or on the bank within easy leaping distance of the water. The male's vocal sacs are on either side of the head and are easily seen. Its croak is a loud *croax, croax, brek, kek, kek.*

Size	Up to 15 cm.
Habitat	Always close to water, in marshes, slow-flowing rivers, reservoirs, etc.
Food	Invertebrates, fish and other amphibians.
Range	Confined to Spain, Portugal and S France, where it is both widespread and often common.
Similar species	Pool Frog (p.186). A similar Marsh Frog, *R. ridibunda*, occurs in E Europe.

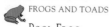

POOL FROG *Rana lessonae*

The smallest of the 'green' frogs, it is nearly always seen close to water, basking on lily pads, floating at the surface or on the water's edge within leaping distance of the water. It is often very noisy, with a call similar to that of the Iberian Marsh Frog (p.185).

Size   Usually 4–5 cm, sometimes larger.

Habitat   Wide variety, but always close to water.

Food   Invertebrates and other small animals.

Range   France, east to the Russian states and S Sweden, and south to Italy and Sicily.

Similar species   Iberian Marsh Frog (p.185) and Edible Frog, *R. esculenta.*

AMERICAN BULLFROG *Rana catesbiana*

A very large frog, with an exceptionally large eardrum. Originally from North America, it has been introduced into northern Italy, where its range is slowly spreading. Its behaviour is similar to the Iberian Marsh Frog (p.185), and the male has a loud call usually described as *jug-o-rum*.

Size	Up to 15 cm, occasionally larger.
Habitat	Close to lakes, slow-moving rivers, ponds and other watery places.
Food	Invertebrates and small animals, including fish and amphibians.
Range	Introduced into N Italy.
Similar species	Iberian Marsh Frog and Edible Frog, *R. esculenta*.

TORTOISES AND TURTLES

Worldwide, there are over 300 species of tortoises, terrapins and marine turtles. They all have a body which is enclosed in a shell or carapace. The shell is usually covered in hard, horny scales, but in some species it is enclosed in a tough skin. The term turtle is confusing: in America it refers to all the species, whereas in Europe it is generally restricted to the marine species.

They all lay eggs, the sea turtles coming to sandy beaches in order to lay. The newly hatched young are miniature versions of the adults, but often more strikingly marked. All species have declined in recent years. The marine species are hunted for their meat and shells, and their eggs are gathered. They are also drowned in fishing gear, and some species swallow plastic bags in mistake for jellyfish. The land tortoises have been collected in their thousands for the pet trade, and they have also suffered from extensive forest fires in the Mediterranean areas.

All turtles and tortoises lay eggs, and when the young hatch they are miniatures of the parents. This is a Spur-thighed Tortoise

HERMANN'S TORTOISE *Testudo hermanni*

This tortoise is distinguished from other European species by having a large claw-like scale on the tip of its tail, and two plates on the edge of the shell above the tail. Like all tortoises it lays round, white eggs with leathery shells; these are often dug up by mammals such as martens for food. They are also killed in forest fires, and have been collected as pets.

Size	Shell is up to 20 cm long.
Habitat	Meadows, farmland, olive groves, vineyards, but usually in areas with thick undergrowth.
Food	Mostly vegetable matter, but also carrion.
Range	Once widespread in S Europe, now only in scattered populations, particularly in Italy and the Balkans.
Similar species	Other tortoises; terrapins are flatter.

SPUR-THIGHED TORTOISE *Testudo graeca*

Similar to Hermann's Tortoise (opposite), but the
tail does not end in a claw, and there is only one
plate on the edge of the shell above the tail. As its
name suggests, it has spur-like scales on its thighs.
Tortoises usually hide during the heat of the day,
but can often be heard as they move slowly through
undergrowth in the early morning or evening.

Size	Shell is up to 25 cm long.
Habitat	Similar to Hermann's Tortoise – usually in thick vegetation.
Food	Mostly vegetation, but also scavenges carrion.
Range	Confined to small populations in warmer parts of the Mediterranean.
Similar species	Other tortoises; terrapins are flatter.

MARGINATED TORTOISE *Testudo marginata*

The Marginated Tortoise is very similar to the Spur-thighed Tortoise (p.191), but usually has a longer, narrower shell, which flares at the rear in older animals. The eggs are ping-pong ball sized. Hatchling tortoises are miniature replicas of the adults, without the flaring on the shell, and are difficult to distinguish from the Spur-thighed Tortoise.

Size	Shell can be up to 50 cm long, but usually under 30 cm.
Habitat	As other tortoises – usually in dense undergrowth.
Food	Vegetable matter and also carrion.
Range	Relatively small area of S Greece and Sardinia. Probably introduced into parts of Italy.
Similar species	Spur-thighed Tortoise. Horsefield's Tortoise (*T. horsefieldi*), imported from Russia, is an occasional escape.

EUROPEAN POND TORTOISE *Emys orbicularis*

Despite its name, this is a terrapin. It occurs close to water, often basking at the water's edge or surface. Usually shy, when disturbed it dives and hides in mud or vegetation. The eggs are laid in a shallow nest on the shore, and it hibernates in mud at the bottom of lakes or ponds. It is generally dark brown or blackish, with pale streaks.

Size	Shell is up to 30 cm long.
Habitat	Slow-moving rivers, canals, lakes, ponds and similar places, usually with dense vegetation.
Food	Mainly small animals and carrion.
Range	Formerly widespread over much of C and S Europe, but increasingly rare in north of range.
Similar species	Stripe-necked terrapins (pp.194 & 195).

193

EASTERN STRIPE-NECKED TERRAPIN *Mauremys caspica*

A predominately green-grey terrapin, with conspicuous stripes on the neck. The carapace is much flatter than that of tortoises. It often basks in the sun, and individuals may congregate close together, by the water's edge. Hatchlings are more brightly marked than adults and have proportionally longer tails.

Size	Shell is up to 20 cm long.
Habitat	Always in or close to water.
Food	Omnivorous, eating small animals and vegetable matter.
Range	Greece (including Crete), north to Bulgaria, and the coast of former Yugoslavia.
Similar species	European Pond Tortoise (p.193) and Iberian Stripe-necked Terrapin (opposite).

IBERIAN STRIPE-NECKED TERRAPIN *Mauremys leprosa*

Closely related and very similar in overall appearance to the Eastern Stripe-necked Terrapin (opposite), the Iberian species is usually darker on the underside. It often basks on the shore, but always within easy reach of the water. The only time it moves far from water is when laying its eggs, which have to be safe from flooding.

Size	Shell is up to 20 cm long.
Habitat	Close to still or slow-moving water.
Food	Omnivorous, feeding on invertebrates and other small animals, vegetable matter and carrion.
Range	Confined to Spain and Portugal.
Similar species	European Pond Tortoise (p.193) and Eastern Stripe-necked Terrapin.

RED-NECKED TERRAPIN *Chrysemys scripta*

Tens of thousands of Red-necked Terrapin hatchlings have been imported into Europe for the pet trade. Although most die, occasionally they survive and grow, and some have been released into the wild. They may be encountered almost anywhere, but in particular in city parks.

Size	Shell grows up to 20 cm.
Habitat	In or close to water, but may wander.
Food	Omnivorous, but mostly invertebrates and other animal food.
Range	Introduced from North America. May be breeding in Italy and elsewhere.
Similar species	Most likely to be confused with stripe-necked terrapins (pp.194 & 195).

GREEN TURTLE *Chelonia mydas*

Rare in Europe, it is mostly found in the Tropics. It was probably once much more abundant, but has declined through over-hunting. It is generally olive or greenish-brown, with mottling or streaking. It prefers warm waters, with extensive beds of seaweed. This is the species used for making turtle soup.

Size	Up to 1.4 m, but usually much smaller.
Habitat	Entirely marine, often in coastal waters, breeding on sandy beaches.
Food	Adult feeds on algae and other marine plants. Hatchlings and young eat small marine animals.
Range	Rare in European waters, but has bred in the Mediterranean Sea.
Similar species	Other turtles.

197

LOGGERHEAD TURTLE *Caretta caretta*

The species of turtle most likely to be encountered in European waters, it is often accidentally caught by fishermen in the Mediterranean. The numbers captured and killed, or drowned in fishing nets, are probably a serious threat to the survival of the species. Like other turtles it returns to sandy beaches to nest, and these sights are increasingly threatened by resort developments.

Size	Up to 1 m, occasionally more.
Habitat	Marine, coming to shore to nest.
Food	Jellyfish, crustaceans and other animals.
Range	Has been recorded from Black Sea, Atlantic Ocean and Mediterranean Sea (breeding in latter).
Similar species	Other turtles.

LUTH (OR LEATHERBACK) TURTLE *Dermochelys coriacea*

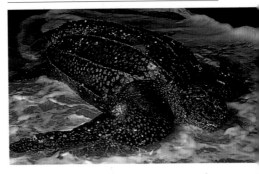

A very large turtle, with five or seven ridges running the length of its carapace. It often occurs far out at sea, and is a regular migrant to Atlantic waters, probably coming from the American side of the Atlantic. It has been shown to be able to regulate its body temperature. It nests on sandy beaches laying table-tennis ball sized eggs.

Size	Up to 1.8 m, and weighing up to 500 kg.
Habitat	Marine, and largely pelagic, coming to beaches to nest.
Food	Jellyfish and other animals.
Range	Atlantic Ocean and Mediterranean Sea (where it breeds).
Similar species	All other turtles have horny plates on the carapace.

LIZARDS

Around 3,000 lizards are known, over 50 of which occur in Europe. They range in size from geckoes about 6 cm long to the Eyed Lizard, which can grow to a total length of 80 cm. Most are agile, the geckoes particularly so; some species have adhesive pads on their toes enabling them to climb smooth surfaces and even hang upside down.

Most lizards feed on invertebrates, but many also eat fruit and other vegetable matter. Some of the larger species, such as the Eyed Lizard, eat small mammals, nestling birds and other lizards. Not all lizards have legs: several skinks have limbs reduced to vestiges, and the Slow Worm and European Glass Lizard are completely legless. A common feature among most lizards is their ability to shed their tail (autotomy); when they are grabbed by the tail the predator is left with it writhing violently. The young of several species have brightly coloured tails, to draw attention away from the head and body. The majority of lizards lay eggs, but a few retain the eggs within the body in order to incubate them.

Green Lizards, like most other species, spend a considerable amount of time basking in the sun, particularly in the mornings

MOORISH GECKO *Tarentola mauritanica*

A gecko with very obvious toe pads. It is usually grey, buff or brownish, and covered with swellings (tubercles); it frequently has some dark bands, particularly on the tail. It is extremely agile, and can run up smooth surfaces, and even cling to a rough ceiling and run upside down. It is mostly active by night and can often be seen hunting around lamps.

Size	Up to 15 cm, including tail.
Habitat	On walls and trees. Most commonly seen around human habitations, often inside houses.
Food	Insects and spiders.
Range	Widespread on Mediterranean coasts, including islands. Also well inland in Spain and Portugal.
Similar species	Other geckoes and lizards.

TURKISH GECKO *Hemidactylus turcicus*

Despite its name, this species is found throughout the Mediterranean, and has spread (by boat) to many other parts of the world. It has prominent tubercles on its back, and the toe pads are short, with the claws projecting beyond the pad. It may make a 'mewing' sound. It is mainly active by night, hiding by day under tree bark or in crevices.

Size	Up to 10 cm, including tail.
Habitat	Drystone walls, olive groves and other dry, rocky areas.
Food	Invertebrates.
Range	Across the Mediterranean area, but rarely more than a few miles inland.
Similar species	Other geckoes and lizards.

AGAMA *Agama stellio*

A large lizard with an extremely long, tapering tail. It is usually seen basking on walls and on trees, and it nods its head. Generally brown and rather spiny, particularly behind the head, the male becomes reddish when excited. Also known as the Hardun, it is probably not native to Europe, but may have been introduced several hundred years ago.

Size	Up to 30 cm, including tail.
Habitat	Olive groves, drystone walls and similar places.
Food	Omnivorous, includes fruit and some small animals.
Range	Confined to Corfu and a few Aegean islands; also on the Greek mainland, near Salonika.
Similar species	None.

CHAMELEON *Chamaeleo chameleon*

A fairly large, slow-moving lizard well known for its ability to change its colouring to match its background. It has a prehensile tail and grasping feet, with two toes forward and two back. The eyes can move independently of each other, and are covered with scaly lids. The Chameleon has an exceptionally long tongue, capturing insects on its sticky tip.

Size	Up to 30 cm long, including tail.
Habitat	Usually in bushes, often in arid areas.
Food	Insects.
Range	Originally from N Africa, it occurs in S Portugal and Spain, Crete, Sicily and a few other places.
Similar species	None.

DALMATIAN ALGYROIDES *Algyroides nigropunctatus*

A long-tailed, slender lizard that is generally rather dark above. The male has an orange-red belly and a distinctive bright blue throat. At close range it can be distinguished from other small lizards by the rough appearance of the scales on the back. It often basks on top of rocks, on branches and similar places, and is very conspicuous.

Size	Up to 21 cm, of which the tail is up to 14 cm.
Habitat	On walls, around olive or oak groves, often in partial shade. Occasionally around human habitations.
Food	Mostly invertebrates.
Range	From coastal Slovenia, south to NW Greece.
Similar species	Most likely to be confused with Common Lizard, which never has blue throat, or Greek Algyroides, *A. moreoticus.*

Spanish Algyroides *Algyroides marchi*

A small, slender, long-tailed lizard. It is usually rich brown above, and often has a dark stripe down the middle of the back. The belly is normally whitish, but is yellow in breeding males. Like other algyroides, it prefers shaded areas, close to water, and is agile, often climbing in trees. It was discovered in 1958.

Size   Up to 14 cm, of which the tail is up to 9 cm.

Habitat   Normally in pine woods.

Food   Invertebrates.

Range   Confined to a relatively small area in Spain.

Similar species   Iberian Wall Lizard (p.220).

207

LARGE PSAMMODROMUS *Psammodromus algirus*

A fairly large, long-tailed lizard, which is often very common. It is usually brownish above, with two pale cream stripes, and reddish-brown around the hind legs; some males have bright blue spots on the shoulders. It is usually found on or near the ground and when picked up may squeak loudly.

Size	Up to 25 cm, of which the tail is 15 cm or more.
Habitat	Usually in wooded areas with thick vegetation, including prickly pear.
Food	Invertebrates.
Range	Widespread across Spain and Portugal, and also in SW France.
Similar species	Spanish Psammodromus (opposite).

SPANISH PSAMMODROMUS *Psammodromus hispanicus*

A relatively small, slender, long-tailed lizard. Although smaller, it is similar in build and proportions to the Large Psammodromus (opposite), but its colouring is more variable – it can be grey, brown or ochre above, and may have spotting, streaking or stripes. It usually occurs in very open arid areas, and when disturbed it runs for a considerable distance.

Size	Usually less than 15 cm, of which the tail is up to 9 cm.
Habitat	Open desert-like areas with only sparse vegetation.
Food	Invertebrates.
Range	Confined to Spain, Portugal and extreme SW France.
Similar species	Large Psammodromus.

SPINY-FOOTED LIZARD *Acanthodactylus erythrurus*

A medium-sized, ground-living lizard with a long tail. The markings are often striking: adults vary from grey to brown, with up to 10 creamy stripes, as well as dark blotches. The hatchling lizards are quite unlike the adults, the body being covered with black and white stripes and the tail bright orange-red.

Size	Up to 21 cm, of which the tail is about two-thirds.
Habitat	Open areas, including beaches and rocky plains.
Food	Invertebrates.
Range	Widespread over Spain and Portugal, except the north.
Similar species	None.

Eyed Lizard *Lacerta lepida*

A very large, green lizard, with a massive head and often bright blue 'eyes' or ocelli along the sides. In the past, animals of up to 80 cm long were recorded, but such large specimens are much rarer now. It preys on insects and invertebrates when young, but the adult eats other lizards, baby mice and nestling birds – almost any animal it can catch.

Size	Up to 60 cm, of which the tail is up to 40 cm.
Habitat	Wide variety of well-vegetated habitats, including farmland, olive groves and vineyards.
Food	Invertebrates and small animals; also some fruit.
Range	Widespread in Spain and Portugal. Also in S France and extreme NW Italy.
Similar species	Green Lizard (p.212).

GREEN LIZARD *Lacerta viridis*

The male Green Lizard has a larger head than the female, and also has a blue throat and chin. Like many other lizards, the hatchlings are markedly different from the adult, being uniformly olive-brown, or with 2 or 4 pale stripes down the back; they gradually become green and yellow as they mature, the mixture often appearing 'beaded'.

Size	Up to 40 cm, of which the tail is about two-thirds.
Habitat	Mainly well-vegetated areas, in hedges, and clearings in woods; frequently basks in morning sun.
Food	Invertebrates, small vertebrates and some fruit.
Range	Most of Europe, north to Jersey, south to N Spain, Italy and Sicily, and E Europe.
Similar species	Other green lizards.

Sand Lizard *Lacerta agilis*

This small lizard is similar in proportions to green lizards. Although it is one of the most widespread lizards in Europe (including England), in the north it is mainly confined to sandy heathland. As this habitat has been largely destroyed in the 20th century, it is now endangered in many areas. It lays eggs, but, in the north, they often fail to hatch.

Size	Up to 23 cm, of which the tail is up to 14 cm.
Habitat	Wide variety, mostly lowland heath in north, but well-vegetated upland up to 2,000 m in south.
Food	Mostly invertebrates.
Range	Widespread in C and E Europe, north to England and Scandinavia; absent from Spain, Portugal and Italy.
Similar species	Other small lizards are generally more slender.

COMMON LIZARD *Lacerta vivipara*

The most widespread and often the most abundant lizard in Europe. Its range extends north to Scotland and the Arctic Circle; it is able to survive in such cold areas by keeping its eggs within the body. By basking in the sun the female incubates the eggs, which hatch within her. The young are born almost jet-black – even the adult is relatively dark – in order to absorb the maximum of the sun's warmth.

Size	Up to 20 cm, of which the tail is up to 12 cm.
Habitat	Very variable, but usually in relatively damp areas.
Food	Mostly invertebrates.
Range	Europe, but absent from most of the Mediterranean area.
Similar species	Other small lizards, particularly the Common Wall Lizard, *Podarcis muralis*.

IBERIAN ROCK LIZARD *Lacerta monticola*

A very variable small lizard, adapted to living at high altitudes with long winters. Although some individuals are brownish and easily confused with other small lizards, others are brilliantly marked bright turquoise green with black marbling; they normally all have a greenish belly. The young are dark bodied, but have a bright turquoise tail for distracting predators.

Size	Up to 21 cm, of which the tail is up to 15 cm.
Habitat	Confined to areas above 1,100 m, often near the tree line.
Food	Invertebrates.
Range	Isolated populations in Spain, Portugal and France.
Similar species	Other small lizards.

IBIZA WALL LIZARD *Podarcis pityusensis*

A very variably coloured small lizard. It occurs on many small islands, and each population has its own characteristics – some are small and slender, others are much darker. Some have white bellies, others pink, grey, orange or white.

Size	Up to 20 cm, of which the tail is up to 14 cm, (usually smaller).
Habitat	Wide variety, including almost bare rock and around human settlements.
Food	Invertebrates.
Range	Native to Ibiza and other small islands in the Balearics. Introduced into others, including Mallorca.
Similar species	May be confused with Lilford's Wall Lizard (p.219), which occurs on Mallorca and Menorca.

ITALIAN WALL (OR FIELD) LIZARD *Podarcis sicula*

Probably the most variable in appearance of all the small lizards, but the only species it is likely to be confused with is the Common Wall Lizard, which normally has some dark markings on its underside. It is highly adaptable, and is found in towns and cities, often in and around human habitations.

Size	Up to 25 cm, of which the tail is up to 16 cm (usually smaller).
Habitat	Very variable: includes road verges, vineyards, town parks and scrubland.
Food	Invertebrates; also fruit and other plant matter.
Range	Italy, Sicily, Corsica and Sardinia, and other nearby islands.
Similar species	Common Wall Lizard, *P. muralis*, and other small lizards.

DALMATIAN WALL LIZARD *Podarcis melisellensis*

A small lizard, which usually has some green on its back, and has rather variable markings. Some have stripes or spots, others have more uniform colouring. The belly is whitish, orange or red, usually without any spots. The hatchlings are brownish, never green. It is mainly terrestrial, although it may climb on low walls and stone piles.

Size	Up to 19 cm, of which the tail is about two-thirds.
Habitat	Generally dry, well-vegetated areas.
Food	Invertebrates.
Range	Only along the Adriatic coast from Italy to N Albania.
Similar species	Other small lizards.

LILFORD'S WALL LIZARD *Podarcis lilfordi*

A very variable lizard that ranges from almost black to a more typical lizard colouring of green on the back and spotted on the sides. The underside is white, orange or yellowish. Black individuals have bluish spots on the sides. It is a remarkably hardy lizard, often living on islands that are almost bare rocks.

Size	Up to 20 cm, of which the tail is less than two-thirds.
Habitat	Rocky islands, with little vegetation.
Food	Invertebrates, and also vegetable matter.
Range	Confined to Mallorca, Menorca and nearby islands and islets.
Similar species	Other small lizards.

IBERIAN WALL LIZARD *Podarcis hispanica*

A small, rather slender lizard, with a rather flattened body. Its markings are extremely variable, but it is usually striped, though in some areas it is blotched. It can be very difficult to distinguish this species from the Common Wall Lizard in the areas where their ranges overlap.

Size	Up to 19 cm, of which the tail is about two-thirds.
Habitat	Generally dry, rocky areas, including roadsides and walls.
Food	Invertebrates.
Range	Confined to Spain, Portugal and S France.
Similar species	Common Wall Lizard, *P. muralis* and Spanish Algyroides (p.207).

SLOW WORM *Anguis fragilis*

The Slow Worm is a legless lizard. It is very smooth scaled and generally dullish-brown (although males may have blue spots); the tail is easily shed leaving it rather blunt. The female usually gives birth to live young, but sometimes lay eggs that hatch almost immediately. At birth the young are like little golden needles, black on the underside.

Size	Up to 50 cm, but usually much less.
Habitat	Generally thickly vegetated areas, often hides under logs and stones.
Food	Invertebrates, including slugs and earthworms.
Range	Across most of Europe, including many islands, except Ireland, S Spain, Portugal and N Scandinavia.
Similar species	Possibly confused with skinks or young snakes.

EUROPEAN GLASS LIZARD *Ophisaurus apodus*

This is a larger relative of the Slow Worm (p.221). It is thick-bodied and, unlike snakes, it has an obvious groove down each side. The skin is very smooth and has a glassy appearance. It is usually found in dry habitats, often basking in bushes, and it makes a lot of noise as it rustles through undergrowth when disappearing from an intruder. It lays up to 10 eggs.

Size	Up to 1.4 m, but usually much less.
Habitat	Dry rocky hillsides, usually with bushes.
Food	Invertebrates, and small animals, including young mice and lizards.
Range	Confined to E Europe, extending north to Istria.
Similar species	Snakes are not as thick bodied and glassy, and do not have a groove down each side.

EYED (OR OCELLATED) SKINK *Chalcides ocellatus*

This large, heavy-bodied skink has short legs and a shiny appearance. The markings are rather variable, but it is often covered with white-centred, black spots on its back – the 'eyes' or 'ocellations' that give it its name. It sometimes burrows in loose soil or under stones, and during hot weather is often active by night. The female gives birth to up to 10 young.

Size	Up to 30 cm, of which the tail is up to 15 cm.
Habitat	Mainly sandy areas, including vineyards and near beaches.
Food	Invertebrates.
Range	Sardinia, Sicily, Greece, Crete and a few other locations.
Similar species	Bedriaga's Skink, *C. bedriagai*, is smaller and fatter, and occurs in Spain and Portugal.

THREE-TOED SKINK *Chalcides chalcides*

The Three-toed Skink is particularly long and slender, with a shiny appearance. The body is often striped and the legs are very short, with only three toes. It is active by day, extremely agile, and so fast that it can scarcely be seen as it moves across the surface of vegetation. The female gives birth to 20 or more live young.

Size	Up to 40 cm, of which the tail is up to 20 cm.
Habitat	Usually in grassy meadows and other well-vegetated areas.
Food	Invertebrates.
Range	Spain, Portugal and Italy; also extreme S France, and on Sicily and Sardinia.
Similar species	No other species has tiny legs.

AMPHISBAENIAN *Blanus cinereus*

At first glance the Amphisbaenian might be mistaken for a rather large earthworm. It is adapted to an almost subterranean existence, and because of its burrowing habits is rarely seen above ground, but can be found under logs and stones, or in the soil when gardening. Sometimes called Worm Lizards, they are not related to either snakes or lizards. The eye is tiny and covered with a scale, and probably only serves to distinguish light from dark. It lays eggs.

Size	Up to 30 cm.
Habitat	Entirely underground in damp soil.
Food	Ants and termites.
Range	Confined to Spain and Portugal.
Similar species	None.

SNAKES

Of some 2,700 snakes worldwide, about 28 occur in Europe. They are all long-bodied and lack legs, though some have spur-like vestiges. The eyes are covered with a scale, but they do not have movable eyelids, unlike most lizards. All snakes are predatory, usually only taking live prey; their jaws are very loosely attached and consequently they are able to swallow relatively large prey. The vipers have fangs which can inject poison. While some species (particularly in Eastern Europe) are extremely dangerous, others, such as the Adder, rarely cause fatalities, and certainly do not justify the widespread persecution they receive. Adders have courtship 'dances' (right) and give birth to living young, although the majority of European snakes lay eggs. Snakes are generally active by day, and often bask in the sun, particularly in the early morning. However, during the hotter months in southern Europe some species are more active at night.

The courtship dance of the Adder

WORM SNAKE *Typhlops vermicularis*

This secretive snake has a very smooth skin, and, unlike most other snakes, does not have enlarged scales on the belly. The head is barely separated from the body (there is no neck) and the eyes are reduced to mere pinpoints, covered by scales. The tail is slightly thicker at the end than the rest of the body. It lays up to 8 elongated eggs.

Size	Up to 35 cm, usually smaller.
Habitat	Mainly open, dry habitats, living in burrows.
Food	Invertebrates, particularly ants.
Range	Scattered populations in the Balkan Peninsula.
Similar species	None.

SAND BOA *Eryx jaculus*

The Sand Boa is the only boa found in Europe. The body is relatively small and stout, with distinctive glossy scales; the tail is blunt. It is well adapted for burrowing in sandy soils and also hunts in the burrows of mammals, feeding on mice and other rodents, which it may constrict. The female gives birth to live young.

Size	Up to 80 cm, usually smaller.
Habitat	Dry sandy areas, including beaches and farmland.
Food	Small animals, including birds, mammals and lizards.
Range	Confined to Greece and adjacent countries.
Similar species	Vipers are also fat-bodied, but have triangular heads.

MONTPELLIER SNAKE *Malpolon monspessulanus*

A large snake with 'eyebrows', which give it a staring expression. It has venomous fangs at the back of the jaw, which it uses to subdue its prey; a bite can cause numbing in humans (occasionally a fever), but this is rarely dangerous. It lays up to 20 eggs, and the newly hatched young may have varying spotted markings down the back.

Size	Up to 2 m.
Habitat	Generally dry rocky places with some thick vegetation.
Food	Mammals, lizards and birds.
Range	Spain, Portugal, Mediterranean coast of France, N Italy, S Balkans and a few Greek islands.
Similar species	No other snake in its range has the raised 'eyebrows'.

HORSESHOE WHIP SNAKE *Coluber hippocrepis*

The pattern of this attractively marked snake is distinctive, and, as its name suggests, there is often a 'horseshoe' or V mark at the back of the head. The young, as in most snakes, have brighter and more clearly defined markings. Although mainly terrestrial, it will climb in bushes, and is often found around human dwellings. It lays up to 10 eggs.

Size	Up to 1.5 m.
Habitat	Dry rocky hillsides, drystone walls.
Food	Young eat lizards; adult eats mammals and birds.
Range	Spain, Portugal and SW Sardinia.
Similar species	None in its range.

DAHL'S WHIP SNAKE *Coluber najadum*

Like all whip snakes, this is a very fast-moving, slender snake. The adult is particularly attractively marked, having a uniform olive body, with characteristic pale-edged dark blotches on the sides of the neck. It is active by day, and mainly terrestrial. When captured it will lash and bite, but it is not venomous. It lays up to 6 eggs.

Size	Up to 1.4 m, but usually under 1 m.
Habitat	Dry bushy habitats, often along walls and roadsides.
Food	Mainly large insects and lizards; also some small mammals.
Range	Restricted to the S Balkans, extending up the coast of former Yugoslavia.
Similar species	None.

WESTERN WHIP SNAKE *Coluber viridiflavus*

A large, slender and fast-moving snake that is aggressive if captured. Larger animals tend to be fairly uniformly dark above and olive below, but the young, and smaller adults, can be boldly marked. Mainly active by day, and terrestrial, but climbs well. It likes a very wide range of habitats, and lays up to 15 eggs.

Size	Up to 2 m, but usually under 1.5 m.
Habitat	Mostly dry and often rocky areas with thick vegetation.
Food	Lizards, snakes, mammals and birds; the young prey on invertebrates and small lizards.
Range	From NE Spain and W France to Switzerland, Italy, Sicily, Sardinia, Corsica and Malta.
Similar species	Algerian Whip Snake, *C. algirus*, introduced into Malta from N Africa. Balkan Whip Snake (p.234).

BALKAN WHIP SNAKE *Coluber gemonensis*

One of the smaller of the whip snakes, similar in appearance, particularly when young, to the Western Whip Snake (p.233). It is most often seen basking in the sun on rocky hillsides, roadsides, vineyards or in bushes or low trees. If disturbed it is often very aggressive, biting if handled.

Size	Up to 1 m.
Habitat	Like other whip snakes: mostly dry and bushy.
Food	Mostly grasshoppers and lizards when young; lizards, birds and mammals when adult.
Range	Former W Yugoslavia, south to Greece, including Crete.
Similar species	Other whip snakes, particularly the Western Whip Snake.

LARGE WHIP SNAKE *Coluber jugularis*

The largest of the whip snakes, this is one of the longest snakes in Europe. It is most often seen basking in the sun on rocky hillsides, or in bushes or low trees. If disturbed it may attack humans, but although it is aggressive it is not venomous. Its range often replaces that of the Four-lined Snake (p.237), especially on islands.

Size	Up to 2.5 m, but usually under 2 m.
Habitat	Like other whip snakes: mostly dry and bushy.
Food	Small lizards and invertebrates when young; mammals and birds when adult.
Range	Balkan Peninsula, except the Adriatic coast and S Greece. Numbers may have declined in north of range.
Similar species	Balkan Whip Snake (opposite) is usually smaller with darker blotches.

LEOPARD SNAKE *Elaphe situla*

One of the most attractively coloured of all European snakes, the Leopard Snake is also one of the rarer species. It is unusual in so far as the adult retains the contrasting markings of the young snake. It is sometimes seen around houses, where it preys on rodents, which it sometimes constricts like a boa. When alarmed it vibrates its tail like a rattlesnake. It lays 2–7 eggs.

Size	Up to 1 m.
Habitat	Usually dry, rocky areas below 600 m.
Food	Rodents, lizards and nestling birds.
Range	Scattered populations in S Italy, Sicily and the Balkan Peninsula, and some Greek islands.
Similar species	None within its range.

FOUR-LINED SNAKE *Elaphe quatuorlineata*

One of Europe's largest snakes and quite heavily built. It usually has four stripes down the back, but has a bold, spotted pattern when young. It prefers a warm, humid environment and although it is rather slow-moving it climbs and swims well. Its food consists mainly of small mammals, but it will raid poultry, constricting larger prey.

Size	Up to 2.5 m.
Habitat	Mostly dry areas, with thick undergrowth.
Food	Reptiles, nestling birds and mammals.
Range	Italy, Sicily and much of the Balkan Peninsula.
Similar species	Aesculapian Snake (p.238) is more slender.

AESCULAPIAN SNAKE *Elaphe longissima*

This is the snake associated with the God of Medicine (Asklepios in Greece, Aesculapius in Rome), and it is possible that its range in the north of Europe was as a result of movement by the Romans. It is large, but quite fast, and frequently climbs in bushes and sometimes even up vertical tree-trunks. It lays up to 15 eggs.

Size	Up to 2 m, but usually under 1.5 m.
Habitat	Generally in dry but well-vegetated areas.
Food	Small mammals, birds and lizards.
Range	C and S Europe, but absent from most of Spain and Portugal.
Similar species	Four-lined Snake (p.237).

LADDER SNAKE *Elaphe scalaris*

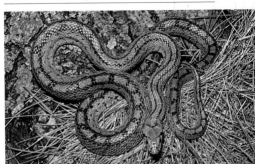

A large snake with a pointed snout. The young are attractively marked with a ladder-like dark pattern on an olive background. They gradually become more uniform in colour, and the markings reduce to two stripes down the back in adults. It can be aggressive when captured, but it is not venomous. It lays up to 12 eggs.

Size	Up to 1.6 m, but usually under 1.2 m.
Habitat	Warm, often stony places, including olive groves and vineyards.
Food	Young eat invertebrates; adults eat mammals and birds, up to the size of young rabbits.
Range	Spain, Portugal, Menorca and extreme S of France.
Similar species	Adult could be confused with Aesculapian Snake (opposite) in north-east of range.

GRASS SNAKE Natrix natrix

The Grass Snake is one of the best known and most widely distributed of European snakes. It is usually green with some barring, and in most parts of Europe it has a yellow or orange collar. It can grow quite large, and is found in a wide range of habitats, but generally near water, where it frequently hunts. It lays up to 50 eggs, in rotting vegetation or manure heaps. It often feigns death when captured.

Size	Up to 2 m, but usually under 70 cm.
Habitat	Usually close to water, but also woodland and some drier places.
Food	Amphibians, fish, small birds and mammals.
Range	Most of Europe, except Ireland and N Scandinavia.
Similar species	Viperine Snake (opposite) and Dice Snake, N. tessellata.

VIPERINE SNAKE *Natrix maura*

The Viperine Snake is superficially like the Grass Snake (opposite), but is even more closely associated with water. It takes its name from its zigzag pattern and its defence mechanism: when disturbed it usually draws its body into coils, flattens the head into a triangular shape and hisses and lunges – imitating the venomous vipers.

Size   Up to 1 m, but usually under 70 cm.
Habitat   Generally near water.
Food   Mostly amphibians and fish.
Range   W Europe and Sardinia.
Similar species   Grass Snake and vipers (pp.245–250).

SMOOTH SNAKE *Coronella austriaca*

This is a relatively small snake, usually buffy brown, with darker blotches or stripes. In Britain it is extremely rare, mainly due to the fact that it lives exclusively on heathland in southern England, much of which has been destroyed during the 20th century. In the south of its range it is found at altitudes of up to 1,800 m. The female gives birth to up to 15 live young.

Size	Up to 80 cm, but usually under 60 cm.
Habitat	Mainly heathland in England; elsewhere more varied.
Food	Mostly lizards and slow worms.
Range	Widespread across Europe, but absent from most of the British Isles, S Spain and Portugal.
Similar species	Southern Smooth Snake (opposite).

SOUTHERN SMOOTH SNAKE *Coronella girondica*

Very similar to the Smooth Snake (opposite), the southern species is slimmer, smaller and generally more boldly patterned. The former, with its more northerly distribution, gives birth to live young, but the Southern Smooth Snake lays up to 7 eggs. When handled it is docile, rarely bites and soon tames.

Size	Up to 50 cm.
Habitat	Mostly dry areas, including rocky habitats and stone walls.
Food	Mostly lizards and geckoes.
Range	Spain, Portugal, S France, Italy and Sicily.
Similar species	Smooth Snake.

CAT SNAKE _Telescopus fallax_

Close-up this snake is easily identified, as it is the only European snake with a pupil that is a vertical cat-like slit, other than the vipers and boa. However, it probably took its name from the cat-like behaviour of stalking its prey. Once a lizard is caught it is held in its jaws for 2–3 minutes, until the venom from fangs at the rear of the jaw takes effect; it is then swallowed head first. It is not dangerous to humans.

Size	Up to 1 m, but usually under 70 cm.
Habitat	Dry, often stony, places.
Food	Lizards and geckoes.
Range	Confined to Balkan Peninsula, some Greek islands and Malta.
Similar species	Most likely to be confused with vipers.

ORSINI'S VIPER *Vipera ursinii*

The smallest of the European vipers, and one of the rarest snakes in Europe, mainly due to persecution. Thick-bodied with a rough appearance, the head is less triangular than other vipers. One of the least venomous (to humans) of all the vipers, it is shy and rarely bites, even when handled. However, it is unwise to handle one, in case it is wrongly identified.

Size	Up to 60 cm, but usually under 50 cm.
Habitat	Variety of wet and dry mountain habitats with good vegetation, including meadows.
Food	Grasshoppers, lizards and other small animals.
Range	Scattered populations from S France, C Italy and east through the Balkan Peninsula. Becoming rare.
Similar species	Other vipers.

ADDER *Vipera berus*

The most widespread viper, its range extends to the Arctic Circle. Its colouring varies, but it usually has a zigzag pattern down the back. The female gives birth to live young, incubating them by basking in sunshine. It is venomous from birth, and can be very aggressive if handled; but, although serious, the bite is rarely fatal to humans.

Size	Up to 85 cm, but usually under 65 cm.
Habitat	Very variable. Drier, more open areas in north of range; up to 3,000 m in mountains in the south.
Food	Small mammals and lizards.
Range	Widespread, often abundant, except Ireland, Spain, Portugal, Italy and most Mediterranean islands.
Similar species	Iberian Viper, *V. seoanei*, is very similar, but confined to N Spain and Portugal.

ASP VIPER *Vipera aspis*

An extremely variable viper, with the typical triangular head, and a pattern that may be a zigzag, stripes or bars. Completely black animals are not unusual, particularly in Switzerland and north and central Italy. The tip of the snout is slightly upturned. Its bite is more venomous than the Adder (opposite), though it may vary regionally, and human deaths have occurred.

Size	Up to 75 cm, but usually under 65 cm.
Habitat	Very varied, from lowlands to 3,000 m in the Alps.
Food	Mostly small mammals, and some birds.
Range	N Spain, France, Switzerland, Italy and Sicily.
Similar species	Other vipers.

LATASTE'S VIPER *Vipera latasti*

This snake has the typical head shape and build of a viper, but is the only viper in its range to have a prominent nose-horn. Its pattern and colouring is similar to other species of viper, the background usually being greyish or brownish. Although it can be aggressive, its bite is normally not dangerous to humans. Like several of the species found in Spain, it is also found in North Africa.

Size	Up to 75 cm, but usually under 60 cm.
Habitat	Generally dry, often rocky habitats.
Food	Lizards, small mammals and invertebrates.
Range	Confined to Spain and Portugal.
Similar species	Iberian Viper, *V. seoanei*.

NOSE-HORNED VIPER *Vipera ammodytes*

The only snake in Eastern Europe with a prominent nose-horn. It is fairly heavy bodied and often very strikingly marked. The male is usually greyish, with a blackish zigzag pattern; the female is brown, with a darker pattern. It is among the more venomous of European vipers, and human fatalities do occur.

Size	Up to 90 cm, but usually under 65 cm.
Habitat	Very varied. Likes to bask in early morning sun, and favours south-facing slopes at higher altitudes, up to 2,500 m.
Food	Small mammals, lizards and birds.
Range	Confined to the Balkan Peninsula.
Similar species	Blunt-nosed Viper, *V. lebetina*, and Ottoman Viper (p.250) are both highly venomous, with restricted ranges in SE Europe.

OTTOMAN VIPER *Vipera xanthina*

A large, thick-bodied viper that lacks a nose-horn. Its markings are very variable, but rarely the typical viper zigzag. The stripe is usually broken into blotches, which are often edged with black. It is a very poisonous snake, and its bite can be fatal to humans.

Size	Up to 1.2 m, but usually less.
Habitat	Wide variety, including arid hillsides, pastures and wetland.
Food	Mammals and birds when adult, lizards when young.
Range	An Asiatic species, also occurs in European Turkey.
Similar species	Other vipers, but they usually have a more zigzag pattern.

Index

Note: Square brackets indicate passing reference. **Bold** entries show groups.

FURTHER READING

Arnold, E. J. & Burton, J. A. (1978) *Field Guide Amphibians and Reptiles of Britain and Europe*. Collins.

Burton, John A. (1980) *Gem Guide Wild Animals*. Collins.

Burton, John A. (1991) *Kingfisher Field Guide to the Mammals of Britain and Europe*. Kingfisher.

Morris, Pat (Ed.) (1984) *Field Guide to the Animals of Britain*. Reader's Digest.

MacDonald, D. & Barrett, P. (1993) *Field Guide Mammals of Britain and Europe*. Collins.